Series / Number 02-048

# Soviet and Chinese Negotiating Behavior: The Western View

## LOUIS J. SAMELSON

*Patterson School of Diplomacy and International Commerce, University of Kentucky*

**SAGE PUBLICATIONS** / Beverly Hills / London

*For information address:*

SAGE PUBLICATIONS, INC.
275 South Beverly Drive
Beverly Hills, California 90212

SAGE PUBLICATIONS, INC.
St George's House / 44 Hatton Garden
London EC1N 8ER

International Standard Book Number 0-8039-0762-1

Library of Congress Catalog Card No. 76-46212

**FIRST PRINTING**

When citing a professional paper, please use the proper form. Remember to cite the
correct Sage Professional Paper series title and include the paper number. One of the
two following formats can be adapted (depending on the style manual used):

(1) AZAR, E. E. (1972) "International Events Interaction Analysis." Sage
Professional Paper in International Studies, 1, 02-001. Beverly Hills and London:
Sage Pubns.

*OR*

(2) Azar, Edward E. 1972. *International Events Interaction Analysis.* Sage
Professional Paper in International Studies, Vol. 1., no. 02-001. Beverly Hills and
London: Sage Publications.

# CONTENTS

# Soviet and Chinese Negotiating Behavior: The Western View

LOUIS J. SAMELSON
*Patterson School of Diplomacy
and International Commerce,
University of Kentucky*

## INTRODUCTION

**Many analysts of the process of international political negotiation** have commented on the apparent unorthodox diplomatic behavior of Soviet and Chinese communist negotiators—patterns of behavior said to be uniquely distinguished by their considerable variance from the norms of traditional western, primarily European-American diplomatic practice.[1] Most significantly, in the numerous accounts of western negotiations with the Soviet Union and the People's Republic of China, there emerges a common portrayal of the rejection by communist representatives of the general customs and procedures of conventional diplomacy. In his early writings, Henry Kissinger (1960: 214; 1957: 318), for example, claimed that diplomacy had become "a form of Soviet political warfare," as they had discarded "the emphasis of traditional diplomacy on 'good faith' and 'willingness to come to an agreement,'" and had chosen to employ diplomatic conferences as "elaborate stage plays which seek to influence and win over public opinion in other nations."[2] In a similar fashion, former American Ambassador Kenneth T. Young (1968: 374) has argued that the Chinese communists had severely revised the western approch to international ne-

AUTHOR'S NOTE: *I am indebted to the United States Air Force for the opportunity to prepare this study while on assignment at the Patterson School of Diplomacy and International Commerce of the University of Kentucky as a Research Associate for the Air Force Directorate of Doctrine, Concepts, and Objectives.*

gotiation by practicing an "adversary diplomacy" characterized by "mistrust, suspicion, the utter lack of any good faith, and the intent to upset and not accommodate 'the other side,' even to widening rather than adjusting a basic conflict." Most importantly, the Soviets (cited in U.S. Senate, 1969b: 80), in claiming to have established "a new type of diplomatic art" appropriate to the interests of "the socialist countries," and the Chinese (Peking Review, 1963: 16), in treating negotiation as a "form of struggle against imperialism," themselves seem to admit to using political negotiations in a manner dissimilar to that of the West.

In view of the considerable commentary on this subject, it is surprising that there has yet to appear a systematic comparative analysis of Soviet and Chinese negotiating techniques, a deficiency which the present study strives to correct.[3] Such an analysis seems especially significant given the intensive diplomatic activities which have characterized American attempts in recent years to adjust political relations with both the Soviet Union and China. Though the achievement of these policy objectives may prove elusive, it would be truly unfortunate if failure were to be attributed to what one American Ambassador (Macomber, 1975: 46) has recently characterized as "the sporadic, hit-or-miss, on-the-job character of a diplomat's negotiating training."[4] It seems clear, therefore, that there is abundant need for a comprehensive understanding of communist diplomacy, and the analysis which follows is intended as a modest contribution to the growing literature on this subject.

It is in their common approach to diplomatic bargaining with the west—strikingly portrayed as deceptive, inflexible, and hostile—that the Soviets and Chinese communists are said to have developed a singularly distinctive mode of negotiation. Yet, though the evidence, as will be shown, tends to reinforce a generally negative assessment of their negotiating behavior, it also has been argued that the intransigent and unresponsive nature of communist diplomacy may have less to do with the actual resolution of conflict than with what Fred Iklé (1964: 43-48) has classified as "side effects not concerning agreement." In this perspective, noted Sovietologist Richard Pipes (Senate, 1972b: 1-2) takes issue with the prevalent stereotypical conceptualization of a unique communist style of negotiation. Pipes claims that it is only when the communists seek objectives incidental to a settlement, such as determining the strength of "their opponents' determination on a given issue, splitting hostile alliances, or influencing world opinion," that is "side effects," that they employ the obstructionist negotiating methods which have so often discomfited scores of western diplomats; but whenever the communists "happen to be interested in a settlement," he concludes, they "act in a traditional manner, efficiently and unfettered by difficulties." This distinction, though somewhat oversimplified, is useful for analytical purposes, for it implies varying communist negotiating patterns which may be situationally-based, and which depart from the obstructionist approach so widely cited by western observers. There may be, in fact, a number of crucial variables affecting communist choices of negotiating techniques. For example, the communist leadership's perceptions of the adversary and his objectives may be critical; if seen as a hostile opponent in a dangerously conflictual relationship with a likely zero-sum outcome, negotiating in a traditional manner may not appear very appealing or rational. Yet, in a different set of circumstances, where the foreign policy objectives of the contending parties are not severely divergent, and where a mutually beneficial agreement may be perceived as possible, the communists might well be prone to employ generally nonobstructionist methods. Other scenarios might be suggested, such as those in which the communists seek agreement but are unsure of their opponent's true objectives, or are fearful of being exploited in their desire for agreement, or are determined to obtain maximum concessions and the most favorable outcome possible; in such cases, an obstructionist approach of varying intensity might be adopted as the most appropriate diplomatic strategy.

It would appear, therefore, that one might expect a variety of situations to elicit a spectrum of communist negotiating responses, ranging in degrees from the traditional, cooperative approach to one of belligerent contention. However, in the general observations of western negotiators who have testified at length regarding their encounters with Soviet and Chinese diplomats, the emphasis is inordinately focused on the obstructionist approach, even when the subject involved negotiations which led to eventual settlements. Thus, in the view of most western observers, it would appear that whatever the ultimate objectives of a specific negotiation, communist representatives have frequently displayed a divergent and especially irritating modus operandi in their diplomatic interaction with the west.

If one presumes some degree of validity in western perceptions of a sui generis communist negotiating approach—as revealed in the surfeit of personal diplomatic memoirs, historical case studies, and academic analyses of communist diplomacy—it should be possible to identify a set of behavioral commonalities in the practices of Soviet and Chinese negotiators. This is not to suggest that those shared techniques which have been distinguished in communist diplomatic practice, and which are identified in Table 1, remain immutable. Negotiations are most properly viewed as dynamic processes wherein the choice of methods does not remain static, but is subject to important forces of change. Alteration in diplomatic style,

## Table 1.

## NEGOTIATING TECHNIQUES COMMONLY ASCRIBED TO

## SOVIET AND CHINESE COMMUNIST DIPLOMATIC REPRESENTATIVES

1. Deception and dissimulation
   a. Deliberate fabrications
   b. Purposeful distortions of reality
   c. Ambiguity of proposals and equivocality in information
   d. Violations of procedural agreements
   e. Non-adherence to traditional concepts of "good faith," "agreements in principle," and the "sanctity of diplomatic agreements"

2. Rigidity and non-accomodation
   a. Prolonged maintenance of inflexible, "all-or-nothing" negotiating positions
   b. Repetitive presentation of unalterable proposals and non-negotiable demands
   c. Unresponsiveness to informational inputs which call into question the logic of a negotiating proposal
   d. Non-reciprocation of concessions, and disinterest in "bargaining"
   e. Unanticipated abandonment of rigid postures, and rapid changes in fundamental positions

3. Hostility and harassment
   a. Excessive reliance on bluffs, warnings, threats, and ultimatums
   b. Rudeness and intentional offensiveness
   c. Impugnation of adversary's motivation
   d. Procedural dominance and manipulation of agenda content and issues
   e. Rejection of interpersonal relations with Western negotiators

for example, may accompany the change of leadership in a government, as some analysts report occurred in the Soviet Union following the Stalinist era, and which is now most clearly associated with the reportedly less obstructionist Soviet leadership style of the détente era of recent years.[5] Stylistic changes also have been observed from conference to conference, and even over time within the same set of negotiations.[6] Similarly, the techniques identified in Table 1 should by no means be considered the sole province of communist negotiators, for many of these same methods seem to be practiced by western diplomats as well. What is most significant here, however, is the general western perceptual view of the methodic and regular employment by Soviet and Chinese negotiators of these techniques, as opposed to their rather unsystematic and infrequent use by westerners. Finally, the use of similar negotiating practices should by no means imply that the U.S.S.R. and the P.R.C. employ a systemically undifferentiated approach to negotiations. Indeed, in view of the widely differing cultural and historical environments from out of which Soviet and Chinese foreign policy has been formulated, one should expect, upon analysis, to find at least some discriminate assymetries in the negotiating styles of the two countries.

Thus, it would be unwise to speak of a specific communist diplomatic style or to attempt to develop an all-embracing universal model of communist negotiating style. The objective herein, rather, will be to document and compare those stylistic features which are generally reported to have characterized Soviet and Chinese diplomacy in their negotiations with the west. Additionally, the analysis will attempt to explicate the various imperatives which may account for the particular methods and tactics used by communist negotiators, examining historical, cultural, and ideological factors, as well as a variety of relevant psychological and social characteristics of the Soviet and Chinese political systems.

## Analytic and Methodological Considerations

Various analytic and research issues emerge in preparing a study of this nature. To begin with, it is obvious that stylistic features represent only one of many variables associated with the complex process of international negotiation. Such other factors as the substance of a specific conflict situation, the policy orientations of the bargaining nations, and the personality, experience, and perceptions of individual negotiators are certainly important considerations affecting the ultimate outcome of a given negotiation. It is prudent, therefore, to examine at the outset the appropriateness and utility of studying negotiations principally in terms of stylistic procedures.

The particular negotiating methods employed by various nations in the resolution—or nonresolution—of contentious issues represent specific "patterns of conflict manipulation and resolution" (Boorman and Boorman, 1967: 145); as indicated previously, the selection of a specific pattern is likely to be based on a variety of factors, not the least of which involves a government's assessment of the overall strategic situation and its adoption of a "grand strategy" to meet the perceived requirements of that situation. Thus, in attempting to achieve specific strategic and policy objectives, the choice of negotiating style may become a critical variable, and as Kennan (1967: 290) notes, "it is axiomatic in the world of diplomacy that methodology and tactics assume an importance by no means inferior to concept and strategy." Unfortunately, western negotiators frequently seem to have been unmindful of the significance of the variations in such methodological patterns of negotiation. As the distinguished British diplomat Sir Harold Nicolson (1964: 68) has commented:

> All diplomatists (the professionals scarcely less than the amateurs) are inclined to assume [erroneously] that their own conception of the art of negotiation is shared more or less by those foreigners with whom they are negotiating.

Obviously, failure to perceive divergencies in method and approach can lead to serious difficulties in achieving an effective resolution of outstanding conflicts.

In many respects, national variations in diplomatic bargaining methods and procedures represent expectations of favorable negotiating outcomes based on historical experience. Negotiators, it may be argued, tend to generalize from their experiences in specific negotiating settings, and "images of past successes and failures are carried over in the minds of negotiators and generally form tactics and strategies" for use in later negotiations (Kertesz, 1959: 133). In this perspective, those nations which experience generally satisfactory outcomes through processes of mutual compromise and accommodation would be likely to develop patterns of negotiation which stress a cooperative approach. Similarly, for those nations which have found success in more aggressive, adversary-oriented methods, it is probable that their negotiating styles would reflect a less cooperative approach.

Whatever negotiating techniques are adopted by a nation, they tend to represent generally recurrent behavioral phenomena which are relatively independent of specific issue content or the idiosyncratic characteristics of individual diplomats. As former American Ambassador Arthur H. Dean (1966a: 34) reports from his extensive experience:

Diplomatic style is a kind of national signature, reflecting not only official policies but also characteristics of the society from which the diplomat comes and the outlook in which he has been bred.

Most importantly, the diplomatic style adopted by a nation "influences heavily the reactions of a particular diplomat and the procedures he will be likely to follow." Thus, in generating appropriate strategies for use in a specific negotiation, it seems particularly valuable for diplomats to develop a thorough appreciation of the methods and techniques likely to be employed by their adversary; and this requires an analytical perspective which strives to isolate systematic patterns of repetitive negotiating behavior.

A focus on patterns of diplomatic style has an even more direct application in the evaluation of the dynamics of specific negotiating situations. As diplomats attempt to feel out particular substantive conditions, explore opposing points of view, and try out alternative approaches to settlement, an elaborate bargaining process emerges. Important perceptual and cognitive features characterize this process, for negotiators must concern themselves with a broad spectrum of behavioral interactions. Thomas C. Schelling (1966: 136) persuasively argues that "the essence of bargaining" rests in such interactions, including "the communication of intent, the perception of intent, the manipulation of expectations about what one will accept or refuse, the issuance of threats, offers, and assurances, the display of resolve and evidence of capabilities," and so on. Schelling emphasizes such techniques as "the creation of hostility, friendliness, mutual respect, or rules of etiquette;" and he concludes that the "deeds and displays" which are the principal characteristics of diplomatic behavior have a major effect on negotiating outcomes. Clearly, an understanding of the important behavioral features of the bargaining process involved in conflict resolution, coupled with the compelling requirements of formulating diplomatic strategies suitable for the conduct of negotiations with the principal communist countries, warrants an investigation into the specific area of Soviet and Chinese modes of negotiation with the west.

There are, however, a number of other analytic considerations affecting this type of investigation, particularly those related to the differing forms of international negotiation. For example, issues of a generally nonantagonistic nature (such as cultural and scientific exchanges and extensions of commercial trade), where the parties may have a mutual propensity toward cooperation, may reflect considerably different stylistic approaches than may occur in the treatment of matters involving conflictual political interests. Although negotiations in the former area have sometimes generated obstructionist communist tactics,[7] the interest in this study rests in the paramount area of conflict resolution, since the essence of diplomatic negotiation is generally seen to involve the peaceful accommodation of outstanding political and military disputes.[8]

Stylistic differences also may be observed in negotiations which are conducted openly as opposed to those which are closed to public inspection. With respect to this distinction, an analyst (K. J. Holsti, 1972: 207) of communist diplomatic behavior reports the following:

> The worst features commonly appear in the open meetings, perhaps because they are used for propaganda, because they fear appearing weak before a public audience, or because they have to show communists that they are sufficiently "tough" with the imperalists. In quiet negotiations, these external pressures are not present, thus allowing Russian diplomats to adopt more moderate styles. These statements would apply to contemporary Chinese negotiations as well.

Similarly, in bilateral talks, where there is only one adversary, the tactics employed by either side may well differ from those used used in multilateral negotiations, where parties of varying ideological persuasion may be present. Additionally, it should be expected that Soviet and Chinese methods in dealing with western countries may differ markedly from those employed in negotiations with governments of nonaligned nations, or, for that matter, with other communist states.

These various distinctions certainly have methodological significance, and may be accommodated in a research perspective which is critically cognizant of their importance. A seemingly more acute research problem would appear to rest in the issue of the basic source data itself, for the most part reports by western representatives of their experiences in negotiating with Soviet and Chinese communist diplomats. Even if one were to presume the accuracy of such subjective accounts, the reports are nonetheless incomplete, since the formal records of the negotiations under concern have generally remained classified by the respective governments. In this regard, official reports of American diplomatic activity available for public use are generally limited to selected dispatches and related papers released by the Department of State in the series *Foreign Relations of the United States,* which are current only through 1949. Thus, as an example, Ambassador Young's major study of the American and Chinese Communist "Ambassadorial Talks" at Geneva and Warsaw from 1953 through 1967 is based entirely on public materials (such as diplomat's memoirs, official statements, and newspaper and periodical articles), but lacks authoritative original source documentation. Young (1968: xi) candidly admits that "naturally there are gaps and perhaps inaccuracies in my treatment. Only the eventual publication of the diplomatic record and access to the documents and primary sources will eliminate these." Although these deficiencies represent important analytic constraints, the recollections of western diplomats often may be more fruitful than official records, particularly since personal reports, unlike public documents, frequently reflect the techniques and substantive issues that occur in the "back channel traffic," that is, the private discussions conducted among senior officials at major conferences. Furthermore, such memoirs tend to provide greater insight into the diplomat's personal perceptions of his opponent's negotiating style than is generally found in sterile official publications.

Despite the apparent utility of the western diplomatic memoir literature, it is important to recognize that these materials reflect significant variations in the perceptual and cognitive abilities of practicing negotiators, and are frequently colored by culturally associated biases and related normative orientations. In the view of former Hungarian diplomat Stephen D. Kertesz (1959: 136), such "sources are not of equal value, and the validity of some is devated, a fact which makes even more difficult the evaluation of attitudes and actions." Notwithstanding such limitations, where better to obtain the documentary data for an analysis of communist negotiating styles than from the reported experiences of western diplomats? Further, were it possible, as it is not, to base the study on comparable Soviet or Chinese reports of their own negotiating conduct (none of which are available), the problem of similar types of distortions undoubtedly would be encountered. Finally, where perceptual and other forms of distortion occur in the available literature, they are most often centered on subjective analyses of the underlying causative aspects of specific negotiating techniques, rather than on the portrayal of the use of such methods—the latter, the principal source of interest for this study. Thus, through appropriate caution in the use of the rich but admittedly subjective memoir literature, and a keen sensitivity to the various other analytic and methodological issues previously described, the following discussion provides an examination of the apparent extraordinary negotiating behavior reputed to characterize communist diplomacy.

## STRATEGIES OF DECEPTION

One of the most commented upon features of Soviet, and to a lesser degree, Chinese Communist diplomatic behavior has been their reportedly excessive reliance on negotiating strategies which employ various measures of purposeful deception. In one writer's (Aspaturian, 1963: 42) acerbic view, for example, Soviet diplomacy has been characterized repeatedly by "duplicity, perfidy, deceit, chicanery, and cruder forms of dishonesty." Similarly, the Chinese have been accused (Vatcher, 1958: 215) of lying "without hesitation" and employing "known falsehoods as part of their tactics." It is said (Nicolson, 1964: 137) that western negotiators "can no longer rely on the old system of trust" that characterized traditional diplomacy, and that in dealing with the communists, it should be recognized that they "will not hesitate to falsify facts and that they feel no shame if their duplicity be exposed." Though such charges may seem to be overdrawn, they represent common western perceptions of communist diplomatic practice, and thus provide a useful departure point for the present inquiry.

The record of international diplomacy, of course, is replete with instances of deception practiced by many states. The fraudulent claim, the misleading cue, and the delusive threat are not uncommon techniques of diplomatic negotiation. Indeed, the frequency of their use suggests that such methods have some functional utility, and specific bargaining situations (such as armistice and arms control negotiations) may present important incentives for deception. At the same time, however, deception carries with it dysfunctional features which may become manifest, as for example, in an opponent's noncommitment to a settlement found to have been achieved through deceit; further, such practice may also do serious harm to future diplomatic relations. Thus, as Robert Jervis (1970: 88) suggests, negotiating states must very carefully "weigh the expected costs of issuing false signals (the probability of being caught multiplied by the disutility that would be incurred in that event) with the expected gains (the probability of successful deception multiplied by the advantage that would thereby be won)."

Despite a recognition of the potential utility of deceptive measures, most western analysts have long proscribed their use on functional as well as normative grounds. For example, the eighteenth century French diplomatist Francois de Calliéres (1963: 13, 330) noted that "the art of lying has been practiced with success in diplomacy;" however, he concluded that deception "actually does more harm than good to policy because, though it may confer success today, it will create an atmosphere of suspicion which will make success impossible tomorrow." Echoing this view, Nicolson (1964: 58) has argued that truthfulness should be the first among all the virtues of an "ideal diplomatist," stating that this should involve "not merely abstention from conscious misstatements, but a scrupulous care to avoid the suggestion of the false or the suppression of the true."

Apart from moral considerations, the essence of such views regarding the efficacy of deception rests in the practical need for states to maintain favorable bargaining reputations. Since it is manifestly in the interest of a negotiating state to be believed, a principal determinant of "whether it will be believed in any given situation is its reputation for telling the truth and doing what it says it will do" (Jervis, 1970: 88). By this standard, the Soviets and Chinese have achieved over the years less than honorable reputations in their diplomatic interaction with the west, for their records are clearly marked with substantive evidence of deliberate lies, broken promises, and violated agreements.

K. J. Holsti (1972: 205), for example, lists a series of Soviet acts which are highly suggestive of their apparent adoption of a "strategy of deception." The list ranges from Soviet failure in World War II to comply with an agreement to permit allied military missions behind Soviet lines to assist liberated Western prisoners, to their violation of an agreement to allow pro-western members to join the postwar Bulgarian and Romanian governments. One of the most blatant cases of such deception involved the 1962 Cuban missile episode wherein Soviet Foreign Minister Gromyko assured President Kennedy that the only missiles in Cuba were defensive weapons rather than (as they proved to be) medium and intermediate range missiles capable of offensive nuclear strikes against the United States.[9] A more current list certainly would include the Soviet-directed emplacement in 1970 of a vast anti-aircraft missile system on the Egyptian-held side of the Suez canal, despite a formal Egyptian-Israeli ceasefire agreement which specifically prohibited new military build-ups. Israeli and American reports (New York Times, 1970) of these Soviet and Egyptian violations were dismissed by Gromyko as "nothing but a fabrication;" the presence of the missiles, however, became well-known during the Yom Kippur War of October 1973, when these weapons frustrated the efforts of the Israeli Air Force to halt a large-scale Egyptian crossing of the canal.

## Indeterminate Deception

Each of the aforementioned cases has involved deceptive practices which are remarkable for their obviousness, and they lend support to former British Ambassador Sir William Hayter's claim (1961: 30) that the

Soviets "have a total lack of inhibitions about truth or consistency." However, other reported cases of Soviet deception involve greater subtlety, and analysis here is less conclusive.

As one example, the Soviets in 1939 publicly entered into apparently serious discussions with Great Britain and France to effect a joint defense treaty against Germany. With the U.S.S.R.'s senior military official, General Voroshilov, heading their delegation, and in an environment characterized by unusual friendliness, the Soviets presented an image of sincere desire to come to an agreement. The Soviets may well have wished such an agreement, but, as it later became known, they simultaneously had been meeting with German representatives. The resultant mutual nonaggression pact between the Soviet Union and Germany, of course, came as an unexpected shock to the British and French; perceiving they had been seriously deceived, this contributed to the suspicion and distrust which marked their relations with the Soviet Union following its later entry into the war against the Axis powers. From a German perspective, the initial Soviet posture of friendliness toward Great Britain and France seemed to serve as a tacit threat to Germany, and may well have provided the impetus to agreement. Thus, it remains debatable as to whether the Soviets were in fact involved in a profound act of deception of all parties, or were merely trying to find some viable alternative to conflict; whatever the case may be, the results proved beneficial, at least in the short run, in achieving a Soviet foreign policy objective (see Langer and Gleason, 1952: 176; Jervis, 1970: 67). Moreover, their employment of a pattern of conciliatory methods for negotiating with the Germans prior to the Nazi invasion of the U.S.S.R. in 1941 represents an important historical example of Soviet deviation from an obstructionist diplomatic pattern in dealing with an adversary. In this situation, the Soviets, cognizant of their limited strategic capabilities, apparently had selected a pragmatic strategy calling for nonprovocation and appeasement, and this strategic choice was amply reflected in their negotiating behavior. Similar departures from the stereotypical pattern, as will be shown, occurred during the Cold War era as well as in the more recent détente period.

In a different type of negotiating situation, Walter Bedell Smith, former American Ambassador to the Soviet Union, reported an experience which represented to him a gross act of Soviet deception, but which in retrospect, has several ambiguous characteristics which call into question the severity of the American interpretation. The incident involved a series of conversations in 1948 between Smith and Soviet Foreign Minister V. M. Molotov in an American-initiated effort to clarify United States foreign policy in the framework of the growing Cold War. Smith (1950: 157-159) notes that the American government, caught up at that time in a heated presidential election campaign, sought to privately and frankly convey "the firmness and continuity of . . . [its] bipartisan foreign policy" and to emphasize "its intention to contain further communist expansion by aggression." Molotov is said to have recognized the value of "informal and confidential communications in establishing a mutual understanding" on these issues, and that "there was no misunderstanding of the confidential nature" of the two diplomats' communications. However, while the American position on the various matters discussed remained confidential, the Soviets publicly broadcast the content of Molotov's statements, erroneously leaving the impression that the United States was conducting substantive bilateral negotiations with the U.S.S.R. without consulting its European allies. The Soviet action was seen by the American government as a deliberate violation of the basic rules of diplomatic confidence—an act which served thereby to disrupt American relations with its allies and to promote considerable distrust in future relations with the U.S.S.R.

Although the American appraisal of Soviet behavior in this instance may be generally correct, Smith's (1950: 157) principal conclusions seem overly stringent, as he claims that the incident

> taught all of us, the hard way, that the men in the Kremlin had carried over into peace the tactics of breaking confidence, of indulging in practices of deception, falsification and evasion which we had always hitherto associated only with relations between enemy states in time of shooting war.

Upon analysis, the harshness of this evaluation seems more to reflect Smith's own personal discomfiture than an objectively balanced assessment of the situation. Smith (1950: 166) admits to having been "surprised and ashamed" of the incident since he had previously disagreed with others in the Department of State who "had anticipated the possibility that the Soviet Government might violate diplomatic confidence in order to seize the opportunity to renew its propaganda 'peace offensive.'" Moreover, he seems to have been particularly fearful of "the confusion and uncertainty which the misinterpretation of the American approach would cause in all the capitals of Europe, and the furor among the American electorate over such a development." Yet, following the prompt release of an official statement by Secretary of State Marshall refuting the implications of the Soviet announcement, the matter resulted in what Smith himself concluded as "at best, only a temporary [Soviet] propaganda triumph." Finally, in referring to Molotov's statement as "a misinterpretation, *unconscious or deliberate*" [emphasis added] of American policy,

Smith (1950: 163) unavoidably calls into question the accuracy of his own negative appraisal of Soviet diplomatic behavior.

There have been various other incidents which raise similar questions regarding the use of deception by the Soviets. In 1958, for example, the United States sent a team of nongovernmental scientists to Geneva, presumably to confer jointly with Soviet scientists and to explore the technical feasibility of various methods and systems for detecting underground nuclear tests. The American delegation to this "Conference of Experts"[10] had not received political instructions from Washington, presumably since the United States viewed the conference as an informal scientific exchange rather than a bilateral governmental negotiation. The Soviet delegation, however, included several diplomats who operated under the formal guidance of their government. Moreover, the Soviets, by arguing that the conference was aimed at selecting the most reliable means of policing a nuclear test ban treaty were thought (Gilpin, 1962: 204) to have been attempting "to manuever their Western colleagues into an implied commitment to a test ban and to *a* particular system by which to police the test ban." Of course, this represented a political issue beyond the authority or competence of the American scientists; yet, the conference concluded with a report reflecting a general understanding of the scientific requisites of an underground nuclear detection system. Later, the United States government discovered that the available detection technology, on which the report was based, was not as accurate as the American scientists had previously assumed. When American representatives attempted to alter the proposed system requirements, they met with strong Soviet opposition. The Soviets claimed that the position reached at the "Conference on Experts" represented an official political agreement by both governments, and the United States found itself accused of "bad faith." In response, the American government implicitly accused the Soviets of deception for having treated an alleged scientific inquiry as a formal diplomatic commitment (Jacobson and Stein, 1966: 75-76; Jervis, 1970: 166-167). However, its case was not wholly convincing due to its failure to stipulate earlier that the conference report did not reflect official American policy and did not represent an official governmental agreement.

Mutual accusations of deception also emerged in November 1962, in the American-Soviet nuclear test ban discussions related to the issue of the on-site inspection of nuclear facilities. The Soviets claimed the Americans had reneged on a commitment to accept a minimum of two to three annual inspections, as opposed to a minimum of twelve inspections which had long represented the official American public position. However,

American representatives, in private talks with the Soviets, had suggested the possibility of a lower number; and Ambassador Arthur H. Dean (1966a: 41-42) admits to having advised the Soviets that the United States might agree to reduce the requirement to as low as eight inspections annually. Though there are no confirmed reports of any mention of a lower figure, there remains the possibility of a Soviet misreading of the private comments of American representatives, particularly since the latter were actively attempting to break a deadlock in the test-ban negotiations. Further, "a seemingly casual remark" purportedly attributed (Dean, 1966a: 44) to British Prime Minister Harold Macmillan in a February 1959 discussion in Moscow with Premier Khrushchev may well have contributed to the misunderstanding which occurred almost three years later. Macmillan is said to have advised Khrushchev to the effect that an established quota representing a "symbolic number" of on-site inspections might prove acceptable for a proposed test-ban treaty, since western insistence on such inspections were seen primarily as a means of satisfying public opinion in the United States. According to Dean (1966a: 44), it was at this juncture that the Soviets "immediately seized on the low number of three as *the* number and rigidly proceeded from there without regard to the available scientific data on which our position was based." Whatever the origin of the conflict, given the prevailing mistrust of the Soviets, the misunderstanding could readily be viewed (Jervis, 1970: 168-169) as a conscious Soviet misrepresentation of the American proposals "in order to commit the United States . . . to a position it knew the United States had never taken."

These latter cases are important in that they reveal a mutual propensity by both the Soviets and the Americans to cry foul even when the evidence is fairly ambiguous. Even more significant is the fact that both sides seem to have exploited opportunities presented by conditions of incertitude and equivocality to attain desired policy goals. This is not to imply in any way that there is no substance to charges of Soviet diplomatic deception. What it does suggest, however, is a need for discrimination in analyzing Soviet negotiating behavior to assure the accuracy of such allegations. That such discrimination is necessary is highlighted by the flurry of sensational public allegations which emerged in late 1975 regarding charges of "gross violations" by the Soviet Union of the 1972 arms limitation agreements (SALT I). Contrary to the weighty congressional testimony of the former senior American naval officer, Admiral Elmo R. Zumwaldt, Jr., who outlined several critical areas of Soviet violation, Secretary of Defense Schlesinger reported (New York Times, 1975a) in December 1975, that "there are sufficient ambiguities in the agreement that one cannot demonstrate conclusively that any particular action on their part is a violation." [11] Secretary Kissinger (New York Times, 1975b) also held this view, claiming that the most serious allegation, and the charge "closest to an actual violation," involved Soviet testing of an antiaircraft radar in an antiballistic missile mode. Kissinger is reported to have stated that the Soviets halted and had not resumed such testing since it was brought to their attention in January 1975—a fairly implicit Soviet admission that this activity may very well have been in violation of the SALT agreements. In the most recent development, administration officials in May 1976, reported (New York Times, 1976) the U.S.S.R. had admitted to a technical violation—"the first clear violation"—of the SALT accords. [12] The offense, dating back to March 1976, involved the deployment of new ballistic missile firing nuclear submarines prior to the completion of the dismantling of some forty older land-based ICBMs, as had been stipulated in an unpublished protocol to the agreements. The Soviets reportedly claimed that the delay was due to poor weather and other technical problems, and promised quick corrective action, but the admission added further fuel to the continuing controversy regarding Soviet deception.

With respect to the Chinese, in contrast to reports of Soviet duplicity, accounts of Chinese negotiating behavior reflect relatively few cases of deceptive practice. This is unexpected, given the long years of Chinese—American antagonism; and though it may be an artifact of the limited available data, it may reflect a purposeful Chinese attempt to avoid such practice when possible. Certain cases, however, deserve consideration, such as accounts of violations of procedural agreements at Panmunjom. In consonance with their North Korean allies, the Chinese reportedly (Vatcher, 1958: 10) "would ask or agree to secret sessions, thus keeping the conversations from the world's communication media, but would at their own whim release the information in their perverted fashion." Vatcher, who served as the psychological warfare advisor to the senior United Nations delegate at Panmunjom, was also highly critical of the Chinese and the North Korean method of making false claims and distorting reality: Vatcher (1958: 10) reports: "The Communists lied without hesitation. They presented fabrications as the truth and challenged the UNC [United Nations Command] to prove them otherwise." Ambassador Kenneth Young observed comparable behavior by the Chinese Communists during the intermittent American-Chinese bilateral negotiations (known as the Ambassadorial Talks) which were conducted in Geneva and Warsaw from 1953 to 1967. Young (1968: 10-11) claims that although

> both parties agreed at the beginning in Geneva . . . that the Ambassadorial Talks would remain confidential . . . , Peking's spokesmen . . . often resorted to press statements or long public announcements,

quite contrary to mutual agreement, presumably to put pressure on the Americans or to embarrass them.

In terms of the traditional concept of the sanctity of diplomatic agreements, the Chinese are said (Young, 1968: 63) to have failed to fulfill the only formal bilateral agreement entered into with the United States: the 1955 "Agreement on Exchange of Civilians."[13] Rather than permit the expeditious return of all Americans desiring repatriation, as stipulated in the agreement, the Chinese claimed that certain prisoners would have to be denied exit until completing their prison sentences. The issue became a matter of a long and frequently bitter dispute in American-Chinese relations, and as Young (1968: 65) reports, the American prisoners were "dribbled out of China" in a piecemeal fashion over a long number of years. In fact, it wasn't until March 1973, almost eighteen years after the agreement was concluded, that the last of the known American prisoners held by the Chinese was released.[14]

## Deception and Ambiguous Agreements

The issue of ambiguity has already been raised in connection with various charges of Soviet negotiating deception, and may similarly be related to certain features of Chinese diplomacy. Central to this aspect of the problem has been the frequent tendency of western governments to rely on so-called "agreements in principle." In traditional diplomatic practice, such agreements have been used to provide general understandings designed to facilitate the conclusion of formal agreements. Though these interim understandings usually lack specifics as to how the eventual agreements are to be executed, they are said (Dean, 1966a: 45) to be "based on the practical steps which the diplomat believes he can carry out in time—perhaps not in every detail, but in broad outline."

A reliance on such understandings, of course, may prove troublesome, particularly when either side may retain divergent views which are not resolved in the final settlement.[15] This would seem to have been a principal factor in the American-Chinese agreement discussed above regarding the mutual commitment to repatriate prisoners, for the final agreement failed to include the precise details (such as numbers of prisoners or timing of release) for its implementation—details which may or may not have been generally understood at the conference table. The mutual misunderstanding and hostility which resulted from the reported failure of the Chinese to comply with the settlement rested in large part on the differing American and Chinese views of the requirements of a very generally worded agreement.

For analytical purposes, the essential problem—and one not readily resolvable—centers on determining whether or not a nation has deliberately attempted to deceive a negotiating opponent through the exploitation of such ambiguous agreements. A review of western negotiations with the Soviet Union during World War II reflects the magnitude of the problem. It well may be true, as Philip E. Mosely (1960: 25) concluded from his personal diplomatic experience during that period, that "the western powers sometimes gained the 'principle' of their hopes, only to find that 'in practice' the Soviet government continued to pursue its original aims." Similarly, it has been charged (Dean, 1966a: 45-46) that the Soviets, cognizant of western impatience for settlement, purposively employed general principles in the wartime negotiations at Yalta and Potsdam to conclude imprecise agreements which they would later be "able to interpret . . . in their own way and act to their own advantage while professing" their full compliance. However, whether those negotiations represented deliberate Soviet deception or differing perspectives of the nature of the issues at stake remains a debatable issue.

A major case in point involves the widely reported failure of the Soviets to comply with what western negotiators (Harriman and Abel, 1975: 412) believed to be the intended interpretation of the "vague and generalized" Yalta provisions for the postwar reorganization of the Polish government (that is, to permit "a broader democratic basis," the "holding of free and unfettered elections," and the right of "all democratic and anti-Nazi parties . . . to take part and to put forward candidates"). Although various analysts (Bundy, 1949; Campbell, 1956) have interpreted the Soviet refusal to support the agreement as yet another case of deceitful noncompliance, conflicting policy objectives and differing perceptual images of the postwar European political structure seem to have been important variables affecting Soviet behavior. In this perspective, factors other than deliberate duplicity require consideration, such as those suggested by deRivera (1968: 363-370), to include: disparate western and Soviet perceptions of the "objective reality" of the Polish issue; contrary beliefs about what "justice" required of each actor's behavior; mutual suspicion and distrust of each other's motivations; and a failure to communicate or sympathize with the interests of the "other side."

## Psychological and Social Factors

These kinds of considerations reflect the prominent attention given by many academic scholars in recent years to the role of psychological and social variables in negotiating situations.[16] There are significant limitations, of course, to the degree to which the innovative conceptualizations drawn from laboratory experiments involving artificially constructed bargaining situations may be applied to the real world of international diplomacy (see Zartman, 1975). Nevertheless, it is fair to generalize (Sawyer and Guetzkow, 1965: 503) that negotiators, like other decision-makers, tend to develop specific attitudes or perceptual images of their adversaries based on prior experiences, ascribed reputations, and anticipated behaviors.

Obviously, such images are subject to change through the negotiating process; indeed, this is said (Deutsch, 1968: 134) to be a principal objective of negotiations—to alter images and change initial biases in an attempt to attain compatability between the values of each side and effect a convergence in views leading to a mutually satisfying agreement. However, since perceptual images brought to a negotiation provide fundamental structures through which incoming information is processed and by which an opponent's positions are evaluated, such images also may be damaging to the resolution of conflict, particularly if they reflect high levels of suspicion and skepticism regarding the motivations and intentions of the other side.

Thus, despite the inherent utility of such established beliefs and attitudes, all too often they may prove dysfunctional by circumscribing the objectivity required in assessing one's adversary. More specifically, psychological research (Allport, 1955: 382) suggests that under conditions of high ambiguity, as are characteristic of international negotiations, individuals tend to turn inward and to rely on their preconceived images rather than to evaluate unprejudicially the statements and behavior of their opponents. Negotiators may come to believe that only their particular side has an accurate perception of the objective reality of a conflict situation, thereby depreciating their opponent's abilities and the likelihood of reaching a mutually acceptable agreement (Fedder, 1964: 113). Perceptual images, therefore, may prompt negotiator rigidity rather than flexibility; and frequently a self-fulfilling prophecy seems to emerge as negotiators "tend to perceive what they expect to perceive" (Jervis, 1970: 132). Further, since these problems are not confined to any single side in a negotiation, such perceptual constraints may produce the well-known (see Hoffman and Fleron, 1971: 317) psychological phenomenon of "mirror-imaging" in which each side employs mechanisms of denying and ignoring its own faults while projecting those faults on the enemy. Thus, while western negotiators may have structured their view of the environment so as to expect the worst from communist negotiators, the communists, as O. R. Holsti (1962: 251) observes, may also be "pre-conditioned to view the actions of the west within a framework of 'inherent bad faith.'"

## Historical and Ideological Considerations

Psychological and sociological interpretations offer considerable insight into understanding many of the reported instances of deception which have been discussed heretofore, and will be useful in the subsequent examination of other features of communist negotiating practice. It is important, however, to recognize that the attitudinal orientation of individual negotiators reflects the general historical experiences and belief systems characteristic of their particular social and political cultures. In both the Soviet and Chinese cases this involves a long history of perceived, if not real, western aggrandizement and hostility, coupled with the commitment to a complex, secular ideology.

Several analysts have stressed the significance of historical factors in accounting for Soviet and Chinese diplomatic deception. A former American foreign service officer (U.S. Senate, 1959: 33),[17] for example, notes that:

> A thousand or more years ago the early Slavic peoples, living in the defenseless steppes of Great Russia and the Ukraine, had to develop a special brand of duplicity in added defense against the onslaught of the central Asiatic tribes. The inheritance of Byzantium must have added to the Russian's own native secrecy. Tartar rule must have taught them even more.

From such a perspective, Soviet deception would seem to have deep historical roots; and discussions of the subject often are related to a communist sense of severe suspicion and distrust of foreigners, as in Kertesz' (1959: 139) view of the "almost pathologically mistrustful behavior" which "became a familiar pattern blurring the judgment of Soviet negotiators on all levels."[18] Xenophobic views are even more pronounced in the case of the Chinese, who are seen (Frolic, 1976: 76) to "have a compulsion to redress wrongs inflicted upon China by the west and by all foreigners." Moreover, both the U.S.S.R. and the P.R.C. experienced long periods in which their governments were isolated from normal diplomatic intercourse with the west; and these historical factors, when joined with the general philosophical framework of their respective Marxist-Leninist orientations, are seen by many analysts to provide the principal determinants of their negotiating behavior.

For example, in Aspaturian's (1963: 43) harsh judgement, communist diplomatic deception is "deeply rooted in Soviet doctrine . . ., a noxious weed whose seeds were sown by Marx and Engels and whose poisonous fruit continues to be harvested by his successors."[19] Such deception, he has suggested, became institutionalized in communist dialectics, representing a "calculated and systematic device to be cultivated, refined, and designed in advance for use as a continuous instrument of diplomacy in dealing with the class enemy."[20] Such hyperbole aside, the major ideological factors here appear to rest in the communists' belief in the inevitable total victory of socialism and their view of the immutable sanctity of doctrinal prescriptions for achieving such victory. As Sir William Hayter (1961: 28) has argued:

> The Russians always negotiate for victory. It never seems to occur to them that the proper object of a negotiation is not to defeat your opposite number but to arrive at an agreement with him which will be mutually beneficial.

Similarly, Young (1968: 375-376) has claimed that "a revolutionary ethic is Peking's only guide," thereby justifying for the Chinese "all expedients and concessions necessary to bring about the eventual destruction of the non-Communist system and the establishment of a world classless society at the final stage of communism." Expressed Soviet views on this subject seem to support this ideological interpretation, as in their discussion (cited in U.S. Senate, 1969b: 77-78) of the "scientific nature" of Soviet diplomacy which is said to be "constructed on the foundation of Marxist-Leninist theory and knows how to use the powerful weapon of a Marxist, that is, truly scientific analysis of reality and the knowledge of regularities of historical development." Such historical regularities, of course, when viewed in their ideological perspective, point to the inevitable collapse of the "imperialist nations;" and this is said (Lall, 1968: 15) to provide the communist negotiator with a deterministic scenario which "he believes the world should and ultimately will follow," and which it is his task to implement.

Communist commentaries on diplomatic practice are frequently cited to demonstrate their ideological justification of deceptive strategies and practices. Lenin, for example, is reported (Leites, 1953: 532) to have disparaged the notion of the sanctity of diplomatic agreements in his widely noted claim that "Promises are like pie crust made to be broken."[21] Similarly, in speaking of the need for flexibility in promoting revolution, Lenin is said (Leites, 1953: 532) to have asserted, "It would be mad and criminal to tie one's hands by entering into an agreement *of any permanence* with anybody." Stalin echoed these views when, in a 1913 speech (cited in Aspaturian, 1963: 49), he stated:

> A diplomat's words must have no relation to actions—otherwise what kind of diplomacy is it? Words are one thing, actions another. . . . Sincere diplomacy is no more possible than dry water or iron wood.

Further, in a rather revealing passage (cited by Aspaturian, 1963), Churchill reports Stalin's comments on the same subject many years later:

> In an alliance the allies should not deceive each other. Perhaps that is naive? Experienced diplomatists may say: "Why should I not deceive my ally?" But I as a naive man may think it best not to deceive my ally even if he is a fool. Possibly our alliance is so firm just because we do not deceive each other; or is it because it is not so easy to deceive each other?

It is not possible to determine the degree to which such ideological principles have been operative in either Soviet or Chinese diplomacy. Since communist negotiators are known to receive extensive schooling in ideological precepts, it is not difficult to understand how one might perceive a direct link between the comments of Lenin and Stalin and the deceptive behavior experienced in western negotiations with the communists. Such western perceptions are further buttressed by the doctrinaire view ascribed (K. J. Holsti, 1972: 204) to the communists that western "bourgeois diplomacy is itself immoral and deceitful," and that communist deception "may be justified as a necessary response to previous duplicity by 'imperialists.'" In this perspective, the Soviets and Chinese may be thought to be applying Machiavelli's (1952: 92-93) well-known observation regarding a prince's need to keep faith:

> A prudent ruler ought not to keep faith when by so doing it would be against his interest, and when the reasons which made him bind himself no longer exist. If men were all good, this precept would not be a good one; but as they are bad, and would not observe their faith with you, so you are not bound to keep faith with them. Nor have legitimate grounds ever failed a prince who wished to show colourable excuse for the non-fulfillment of his promise.

Notwithstanding the admitted significance of such ideological considerations, it would seem inaccurate to impute a primacy to ideology as a determinant of communist diplomacy. The Soviets and the Chinese, like other nations, have conventional interests in promoting their national objectives; and where matters of substance are concerned, it may be argued that ideological considerations become less significant than the pragmatic achievement of policy objectives. Though historical and ideological factors certainly contribute to negative perceptual orientations and resultant deceptive practices, it is essential to recognize that such factors alone "will not necessarily impede successful negotiations where . . . other conditions of agreement are present" (Kohler, 1958: 904). Thus, when a particular agreement is perceived by all parties as serving their interests, negotiations with the Soviets or Chinese may well prove successful, as indeed has been the case in numerous post-World War II agreements. However, the practical problem is far more complex for both the western diplomat and the academic analyst, for it requires an accurate determination—not readily achievable—of the precise preconditions which must prevail to elicit co-operative communist negotiating behavior.

In summary, there appear to be multi-determinant sources underlying the "strategy of deception" imputed by many western analysts to Soviet and Chinese communist diplomacy. Whatever the specific nature or combination of those sources—whether psychological, historical, ideological, or simply pragmatic, and regardless of the accuracy of western perceptions—the important consideration in all of this is that in the reality of diplomatic negotiation, the "opponent" may view the strategy as purposeful. Deception, therefore, is seen—rightly or wrongly—as a fundamental technique of communist diplomacy requiring an appropriate and adequate response; and unfortunately, this view contributes circularly to the mutual distrust and antipathy which so often has characterized western negotiations with the communist states.

## STRATEGIES OF INFLEXIBILITY

Another set of stylistic features commonly imputed to Soviet and Chinese communist diplomats involves their reputed maintenance of rigid and nonaccommodating positions in negotiations with their western counterparts. The diplomatic memoir literature is filled with numerous reports of communist implacability, their distaste for compromise, and their apparent preference for prolonging negotiations through a repetitive reiteration of seemingly unalterable proposals. Yet, the literature also reveals many cases in which communist negotiators have altered substantially their negotiating positions and entered into the adjustive and accommodating processes normally associated with diplomatic bargaining. These discrepant aspects of communist negotiating practice seem to suggest the adoption of strategies of inflexibility to aid in the achievement of foreign policy objectives, and analytical consideration should be given to both the sources and the utility of these diplomatic techniques.

### Structural Constraints on Communist Negotiators

Several variables appear to be associated with the issue of communist diplomatic inflexibility, a principal one of which seems to be related to the degree of authority delegated to the communist negotiator. Many observers of Soviet and Chinese diplomacy suggest that communist negotiators, contrary to general western practice, are not free to act as relatively independent agents of their governments. Ambassador Young (1968: 342) claims, for example, that an American negotiator "may and often does, draft his own instructions, receives the Presidential mandate to proceed at his own discretion within broad terms of reference, and goes out to conduct the negotiation on his own authority." Although this may be overstating the American case, communist negotiators generally seem to lack all such prerogatives (Mosely, 1960: 37), and there is a general consensus among western observers that Soviet and Chinese diplomats are severely limited in even the fundamental areas of procedural matters, let alone in such activities as the formulation of official negotiating positions or the drafting of initial agreements. Such constraints, of course, seriously restrict their ability to interact openly with their western counterparts in a mutual exchange of views and in the traditional give and take of diplomatic bargaining. As K. J. Holsti (1972: 206) claims, communist negotiators simply cannot "respond immediately to their opponents' proposals or . . . make any changes to their own bargaining positions—even to the point where they have refused to agree to the punctuation on a communiqué summarizing the day's proceedings."

These restrictions on the authority of communist negotiators may be traced in part to the foreign policy-making process within the U.S.S.R. and the P.R.C. Though both countries maintain ministries of foreign affairs, these organs and the men associated with them are not thought to have substantial input into the actual formulation of foreign policy. For example, neither the present Soviet Foreign Minister Andrei A. Gromyko nor his Chinese counterpart, Ch'iao Kuan-hua, are members of their respective Communist Party Politburos. Lacking membership in the elite decision-making structures of their countries, these senior diplomatic officials as well as other lower-ranking communist negotiators appear to serve primarily as diplomatically-accredited bureaucrats, functioning as implementers of policy under the specific directions of the highest echelons of political leadership in their countries. As Kertesz (1959: 141-142) argues:

> A Soviet representative executes instructions in the strictest sense . . . [for] he is aware of the weak power position of a diplomat in the Soviet state organization and accepts with grim determination the set of ideas, values, and methods imposed by ruling-party circles [see also Hayter, 1961: 23; and U.S. Senate, 1972b: 4].

There is even evidence that authority at the very top of the ruling hierarchy may be constrained by similar internal political considerations.

Nitze (1974: 143), for instance, reports that during the extensive SALT I discussions, Soviet Party Chairman Brehznev "had withdrawn positions he had previously agreed to on grounds that the Politburo had not concurred." It is these sorts of political limitations which account for Mosely's (1960: 5, 9) critical view of the Soviet negotiator as "a mechanical mouthpiece for views and demands formulated in Moscow," and his assertion that:

> Until Moscow has sent instructions, they can say nothing at all, for they may fail to express the exact nuance of thinking or intention which has not yet been formulated at the center, and transmitted to them. After Moscow has spoken, they can only repeat the exact formulation given to them and no variation may be introduced into it unless Moscow has sent the necessary further instructions.

There are cases, however, which seem to suggest that this western perception of the limitations on the independence of action of communist negotiators may not be wholly appropriate, and that a posture of communist inflexibility may be used as a dynamic for eliciting greater concessions from one's opponent than might otherwise be achieved. The presumption of an immutable negotiating position dictated by the demands of an external higher authority might serve to prompt western negotiators to dimiss certain otherwise desirable options and proposals as unacceptable, whereas a sustained bargaining stance might induce communist compliance. This latter point has been highlighted by one member of the United States SALT I delegation, William Van Cleave. Testifying before a Senate subcommittee, Van Cleave (U.S. Senate, 1972a: 203) was particularly critical of the delegation's disposition to pre-assess the "equity and acceptability to the Soviets" of all American proposals. Claiming that "'negotiability' was more important than whether our positions conformed to any clear strategic policy or objectives," Van Cleave concluded that American proposals during SALT I were "not maximum starting positions at all, but were designed to be acceptable largely as they stood once explained to the Soviets."[22] Thus, desirous of eliciting Soviet compliance, and perceiving—whether correctly or not—an inflexibility in the Soviet position, the Americans are said to have severely delimited their potential options.

An interesting account by Acheson (1961: 14) of an earlier period of American-Soviet negotiations suggests that communist negotiators may be endowed with greater authority than is generally presumed, and may be prepared to make accommodations despite their maintenance of seemingly unyielding positions. In 1949, during the Conference of Foreign Ministers on German and Austrian questions, rail traffic to Berlin had been halted, ostensibly due to a labor strike on the Soviet controlled German railroad. Notwithstanding Soviet disclaimers of responsibility and their adamant view that this problem had to be disassociated from the principal issues under consideration, the British, French, and American ministers viewed the strike as a Soviet induced measure to exert pressure on the west to accede to Soviet claims on the substantive matters of the conference. Consequently, they joined in demanding Soviet support for ending the rail strike or face jeopardizing the entire discussions. Acheson reports that although Soviet Minister Vyshinsky at first strongly refused, after "seeing that we were quite serious about ending the conference, [he] reversed his position on the basis of new information just received"—new information that Acheson notes was thought by some to "have been an invisible note brought by an invisible pigeon." Within three days, "all the problems of Berlin traffic" were resolved, presumably because the Soviets had a greater interest in continuing the overall negotiations than impeding them on a tangential issue.

In view of such reported behavior, it would seem incorrect to conclude, as did one former American foreign service officer (U.S. Senate, 1959: 32) that communist delegates "are only office boys bound by instructions from which they cannot budge," for they must enjoy some degree of flexibility, however limited, in order to conduct diplomatic negotiations for their country. Yet, most westerners who have participated in negotiations with the Soviets and Chinese report an extreme reluctance on the part of the communist negotiator to act without receiving explicit approval for his activities from above. Thus, Soviet diplomats are said (Kertesz, 1959: 149, 139) "to often give the impression that they are automata," thoroughly "dependent on final authority even in minor matters." Equivalent comments emerge from reports of Chinese behavior. During the Korean armistice talks, for instance, Vatcher (1958: 218) claimed that:

No agreement was forthcoming, nor could be expected to be forthcoming, until some higher authority approved it. If the UNC [United Nations Command] made a concession as a *quid pro quo* to a like Communist concession, someone would leave the tent and return in about ten minutes with an answer obviously from higher authority.

Explanations for this phenomena, apart from the issue of the hierarchical nature of communist policy-making, have been seen to rest in bureaucratic and ideological imperatives. Mosely, for example, suggests that the risk of reprimands or even expulsion from the diplomatic service for altering, even slightly, one's specific instructions, helps account for the apparent reluctance of a communist negotiator to act independently, and compels him to adhere to a rigid and intransigent position. In this view, even informational inputs which call into question the fundamental logic of a communist negotiating proposal must be cast aside, for as Mosely (1960: 29) argues, the communist negotiator is constrained to avoid any potential accusation of "giving undue weight to the viewpoint of another government and thus of 'falling captive to imperialist insinuations.'" In other words, to compromise—to "give up a demand once presented, even a very minor or formalistic point"—may suggest the negotiator has become "subject to an alien will" and thereby raise questions as to his overall ideological commitment and loyalty (Mosely, 1960: 32).

Harriman, among others, seems to have been very much aware of these factors in dealing with the Soviets. In one reported case (Acheson, 1961: 92-93), he advised Acheson never to rely on verbal proposals, for he felt the Soviet negotiators would never send them to Moscow; to do so would open "the sender to charges of being impressed by what we said." Thus, Harriman advocated the use of written proposals, for if the Soviet diplomat were to suppress such material, "he would be assuming a responsibility which also could lead to criticism."[23] Despite such strategems, it is clear that having to deal with communist negotiators in such a manner presents serious impediments to successful negotiations. Furthermore, apart from the problem of achieving agreement, there lies the issue of the usual intelligence reporting function performed by diplomatic personnel—a function severely deprecated in an atmosphere where the communist negotiator is perceived (Mosely, 1960: 50) to be serving "as a block to the transmission of foreign views and sentiments, rather than as a channel for communicating them to his government."[24] In sum, it would appear that the communist negotiator, under varying degrees of governmental compulsion, ideological orientation, and personal fear of failure, may often be compelled to comit himself to the "all-or-nothing" approach which so frequently has been reported to characterize communist diplomacy.

The aforementioned observations seem to be reinforced by Young's (1968: 342) assertions regarding the Chinese negotiator who, in his view, "may be expected predictably to stick to the letter of his instructions meeting after meeting, chiché after cliché, with no flexibility whatever;" however, Young introduces a further, and somewhat disparate dimension of this issue, when he reports that "without the slightest indication of a contradictory shift," the Chinese negotiator "may suddenly read out a new position, dictated by the flexible policymakers in Peking, totally different from what he had been saying all along."[25] Soviet diplomacy reportedly also has been characterized by such seemingly incongruous changes in negotiating positions. Kohler (1958: 910), in describing his personal experiences, has stated:

> More than once . . . we have engaged in lengthy, laborious, acrimonious, and seemingly hopeless negotiations with the Soviet Government on particular issues, have talked for months and years without any sign of progress, and then have suddenly found the Soviet Union ready to come to terms within a matter of hours.

While such unanticipated changes and apparent reversals of fundamental negotiating positions may prove disconcerting to unprepared western diplomats, their occurrence is of considerable significance, for it is generally at such points that agreement becomes feasible. Obviously, the "seemingly hopeless negotiations" of which Kohler speaks, reflect not only communist intransigence, but also western unwillingness to meet communist demands. In such situations, should the communist leadership be truly desirous of achieving a settlement, and if it is convinced that its diplomatic representatives have elicited the maximum in concessions from its adversary, it should not be surprising that they would adopt a conciliatory and accommodative posture. These factors, for example, may have been present during the conclusion of the nuclear test-ban negotiations in 1963. Harriman (1971: 92-93) has pointed out that the rigid Soviet position on arms control requirements throughout the formal discussions which had begun in late 1958, led western observers to believe that the 1963 negotiations would take many months before a settlement might be reached; in actual fact, the outstanding issues were resolved and agreement achieved within two weeks after Harriman began his discussions with Khrushchev in Moscow. In this instance, previous Soviet intransigence may well have served to move the United States to make various concessions desired by the Soviets, although Harriman suggests the result was a combination of "pressure on the Soviets" as well as Khruschev's having "made up his mind he wanted an agreement and was going to make every effort to come to terms." Whatever the reason, such reports suggest that the inflexibility so frequently perceived as characteristic of Soviet and Chinese negotiating behavior tends to overshadow their not infrequent willingness to alter positions, enter into accommodative bargaining, and resolve conflictual matters. This, of course, leaves the western negotiator with the considerable problems of determining if, and when, a given negotiation may lead to such resolution, as well as what, if anything, he might be able to do to promote such an outcome.

## Restricted Informational Interchange and Nonaccommodation

One of the most difficult features of any diplomatic negotiation involves the making of accurate assessments of the objectives being sought by one's opponent. This is particularly true of negotiations where side effects (such as propaganda, posturing, intelligence gathering, and so on) may appear to be equally, if not more important goals than those of reaching settlements on conflictual issues. While such side effects seriously complicate the issue, the problem is usually ameliorated through a preliminary exchange of information which may provide some awareness of an opponent's commitment to the achievement of agreement, and some understanding of the nature of the specific requirements and instructions under which he is functioning. Thus, in the early stages of a negotiation, each side may attempt to influence the other with claims and counter-claims, charges and counter-charges, threats and counter-threats, and so on; yet, throughout this preliminary process, each side has a major concern in determining the real interest of the other in adjusting differences and effecting agreement, as well as assessing the degree to which initial bargaining positions may be inflated and include areas subject to eventual adjustment.

Such determinations are reported to be quite difficult for westerners involved in negotiations with the Soviets and Chinese. For one thing, as Mosely (1960: 7, 11) claims, the initial problem may be "to discover whether the representatives have any instructions at all," let alone to assess the nature of their bargaining position. He reports that at certain conferences, it was clear that the Soviet delegation had no specific instructions other than "not to commit itself to anything or sign anything," but merely to "report back." In such a situation, the process of communication and information exchange would appear to be restricted and unidirectional with little opportunity for discerning communist objectives and intentions.

As noted previously, however, the more common case seems to be one in which the communists are thought (Mosely, 1960: 16) to be "bound by detailed instructions rigidly pressed." Although this approach might appear to be more useful in assessing communist goals, the severe secrecy attendant to their negotiating behavior, reportedly far exceeding that of western diplomacy, severely constrains the opportunity to appraise objectively their operational range of negotiating positions. This secrecy may be carried to such extremes that even the communist delegation itself may not be privy to the possible compromises that its government is prepared to endorse; and "the wall of secrecy" surrounding communist negotiating positions thereby makes it especially difficult to ascertain how firmly a given position may be held "and what sort of modifications in the western position might lead to agreement" (Iklé, 1964: 227).

Such secrecy frequently extends beyond general negotiating positions into specific details involving substantive matters under consideration. In his quasi-official account of the American-Soviet Strategic Arms Limitation Talks, John Newhouse (1973: 56, 192) reports, for example, that the Soviet civilian negotiators, including Vladimir Semenov who headed the delegation, knew relatively little about the characteristics, numbers, and locations of Soviet strategic weapons. According to Newhouse's sources, the Soviets had to rely "to a great degree" upon Soviet arms information provided by American delegates. Of course, this caused considerable consternation among the Soviet military representatives, one of whom reportedly "took aside a U.S. delegate and said there was no reason why the Americans should disclose their knowledge of Russian military matters" to the Soviet civilian representatives since such information was "strictly the affair of the military." This incident also suggests the need for reassessing the common western perceptions of a tightly controlled, hierarchically structured, "unitary, rational actor" model of communist decision-making. There is every reason to believe that communist governments, like all large scale organizations, must deal with conflicting and competitive internal institutional groupings, and that resultant policy orientations and strategic decisions are the product of very complex bureaucratic and organizational dynamics. The considerable political changes which have repeatedly accompanied the succession process in Soviet leadership since Stalin's death in 1953, and the continuing internal struggles among Chinese radicals and moderates so widely noted by western Sinologists, illustrate the obvious significance of the "bureaucratic politics" variable (Allison, 1971) in appraising communist negotiating methods and positions.

The close veil of Soviet and Chinese negotiating secrecy has often been thought to represent their deliberate attempt to lead negotiating opponents to believe there is only one communist position—the initial one. It has been argued frequently that neither communist government seems to perceive diplomatic negotiations in the traditional western vein, as instruments for bargaining, accommodation, and the adjustment of differences. In the severe view of a former American foreign service officer (U.S. Senate, 1959: 33) for example:

> To a Soviet the act of negotiation . . . means trying to do one's enemy in. It means trying to achieve by conference the same end which otherwise might be sought by armed force, subversion, propaganda, or other means. A Soviet looks upon negotiations as a method to achieve gain, not as a method to adjust differences.

Thus, a fundamental difference in negotiating approach is said (Dean, 1966a: 43) to prevail—one in which the communists thoroughly reject principles of compromise, and view "unilateral concessions by the west" not as a means of "stimulating reciprocal concessions," but rather as causes of "suspicion and concern" which are most properly taken "as a sign of the other side's weakness."

As in the various analyses of communist deception, ideological imperatives are seen to be involved in the repudiation by the Soviets and Chinese of adjustive measures in their negotiating styles. Thus, it is claimed (Mosely, 1960: 34) that the communists, "trained to assume the ill-will of the 'capitalist environment,'" reject suggestions of compromise and good will, perceiving western concessions as indicative either of the greater strength of communist principles or as attempts at deceptive treachery.[26] Such an attitude is reinforced by a remarkable and widely cited statement of former Soviet Premier Khrushchev (U.S. Dept. of State, 1959: 307) regarding western proposals on the eve of a Foreign Ministers' Conference in 1959 at Geneva:

> They say: "With the U.S.S.R. one must negotiate as follows: concession for concession!" But that is a huckster's approach . . .! We do not have to make any concessions because our proposals have not been made for bartering. . . . Those who really strive for peace must not use methods of petty bargaining in the talks.

Young (1968: 375) reports a similar refusal by the Chinese to participate in accommodative, adjustive bargaining; in his view, the Chinese negotiator

> is preconditioned to consider American overtures and genuine compromises inconsistent with imperative struggle and inevitable defeat of the United States government. He takes for granted from incessant indoctrination that any concession or concilliatory gesture by Washington is nothing but sham and evidence of weakness.

Presuming for the moment the accuracy of these appraisals, the Soviet and Chinese willingness to prolong negotiations interminably becomes more understandable; conference sessions provide them with a means of repetitively presenting unwavering positions which they are convinced are ideologically sound, fully logical, and thoroughly correct. The widely reported "marathon" sessions, which may delay proceedings for almost endless periods, and which so frequently have characterized western negotiations with the communists, thus may have their roots in the ideological perception that victory is on the side of the revolution—the communist side. As Acheson (1961: 103) comments, the prolongation of a diplomatic conference represents "a tactic prescribed by Lenin to delay the crisis while demoralizing and weakening the enemy." Of course, other factors may also be at work, since such extensive and repetitive bargaining sessions may also be related to the general lack of discretionary powers permitted the communist negotiators, as previously discussed; in other words, these "long-talking" sessions may reflect a process of stalling—of marking time—while awaiting further instructions on how to proceed.

However one accounts for such communist negotiating tactics, it is apparent that the western diplomat, generally eager to conclude negotiations as quickly as possible, is placed at a serious psychological disadvantage when faced with such delay and intransigence. Former American Ambassador U. Alexis Johnson's (U.S. Dept. of State Bul., 1963: 277) observations on this subject are instructive:

> During the almost four years that I was negotiating with the Chinese Communists at Geneva, between 1954 and 1958, what I found *most annoying and frustrating* was their supreme self-confidence that they need make no concessions of any kind and that if they just waited long enough, we would be forced to make all the concessions to them. [emphasis added]

Chinese behavior here suggests their "belief that perseverence will ultimately pay off and that a continuous, infinitesimal approach to an objective is ultimately equivalent to its attainment;" thus, as a study of the Chinese "national character" concludes (Boorman and Boorman, 1967: 151), they seem to believe that "given even a feeble but sustained effort over a long enough period of time, success in realizing any goal, no matter how remote, is certain." The idea, of course, is that such delay may so exhaust or provoke one's adversary that he "will be willing to make concessions that he would otherwise not have made [primarily] in order to have a 'successful' conference" (Dean, 1966a: 145). Thus, western works dealing with the problems of negotiating with the Soviets and Chinese almost invariably call for patience, strength of conviction, and a commitment to fundamental objectives which should never be sacrificed (see Steibel, 1972: 40; Mosely, 1960: 36; Iklé, 1964: 253-255; and Young, 1968: 388-390).

## Imperatives to Accommodation

The portrayal which emerges from many western analyses of the Soviet and Chinese communist negotiator as a rigidly disciplined, self-righteous, and wholly intransigent diplomat unwilling to engage in any form of adjustive bargaining in interaction with western negotiators seems to be severely overdrawn. As already noted, both the Soviets and Chinese have been known to surprisingly alter their positions after protracted discussions; and the diplomatic record reflects numerous and significant agreements that have been achieved as a consequence of a mutual conciliation of differences. Analyses (U.S. Senate, 1970) of the negotiations which led to such various settlements as the elimination of the Soviet influenced Pishevari regime from Northern Iran, the Austrian State Treaty, the Korean Armistice, and the broad array of arms control agreements effected since the advent of the "détente era"—while indicative of strongly held communist negotiating positions—reveal a disposition by the communists to eventually agree to western proposals contrary to their own, and to make the necessary concessions required to achieve jointly desired objectives. In fact, a quantitative analysis (Jensen, 1963: 527) of American-Soviet negotiations from 1946 to 1960 on the issue of disarmament found that, contrary to expectations, the Soviets generally proved more willing to make concessions than the Americans. How then to explain such behavior which seems to contradict the common perceptions of the unyielding and inflexible communist negotiator?

One source of explanation rests in communist doctrine which, counter to what might be expected (particularly in view of what has been cited earlier on this subject), is not unalterably opposed to the conciliation of differences with one's ideological adversaries. Communist ideological perspectives are often seen (Lall, 1966: 275) as endowing the Soviets and Chinese with "an unbreakable sense of self-righteous assurance," thereby reinforcing their intractability; yet, the communist orthodoxy contains several explicit endorsements of accommodative behavior. Although Lenin, for example, reportedly admitted (Leites, 1953: 501) that "concessions . . . mean paying tribute to capitalism," he went on to claim that by such means, "we gain time and gaining time means gaining everything." In Lenin's view (Leites, 1953: 531), political concessions could be made, but only on a quid pro quo basis, when "we receive in return more or less equivalent concessions," a policy reinforced in Stalin's 1927 comment (Leites, 1953: 531) addressed to the "capitalist states"; "If you give us something, we give you something."[27] Similarly, Mao Tse-tung (1967: 214), reiterating the argument of Lenin that "to fall back the better to leap forward," asserted that "to regard concessions as something purely negative is contrary to Marxism-Leninism." Mao, in fact, argued that compromise has a positive instrumental value in advancing the communist cause:

When we make concessions, fall back, turn to the defensive, or halt our advance in our relations with either allies or enemies, we should always see these actions as part of our whole revolutionary policy, as an indispensable link in the general revolutionary line, as one turn in a zigzag course.

The constant and readily apparent theme which runs throughout these comments focuses on the potential advantages to be gained by the granting of concessions. As such, conciliatory communist measures, when they do occur and when they are recognized, tend to be dismissed by many western analysts as merely duplicitous tactics designed to exploit western weakness and advance communist objectives. Such analysts seem unwilling to grant the Soviets or Chinese a genuine interest in the amelioration of differences through mutual accommodation, possibly because "it is cognitively inconsistent . . . to think of people we dislike and distrust making honest, conciliatory moves" (Osgood, 1960: 341). Of course, the same might be said of the communist perception of western compromises, again illustrating the psychological "mirror-image" phenomenon mentioned earlier. It is instructive to examine the ways in which concilatory acts by the Soviets and Chinese have been viewed in western analytical literature.

It has been suggested, for example, that the communists enter negotiations with deliberately distorted and extreme positions. This approach, it is often argued, provides them with an opportunity to play up their claimed grievances, harass their opponents, and elicit conciliatory responses, while being prepared to make their own concessions at an appropriate point in the negotiating process. In short, communist negotiating positions are said (U.S. Senate, 1972b: 14) to be "weighted down with . . . unrealistic demands" which can be given up readily with no real loss of advantage in order to obtain substantive concessions from an opponent. In this perspective, compromise is seen (Kulski, 1964: 596) as a purposeful tactic designed to compel one's opponent "to make greater concessions than he would otherwise have made and yet feel that the achieved settlement is a sound one."

In a somewhat different vein—one in which compromise is seen less as a tactical ploy than as a forced retreat—Acheson (1969: 275) has argued that the communists will only abandon a fixed position "when and if action by the opponent demonstrates their position to be untenable." The British scholar Leopold Labedz (U.S. Senate, 1973: 61) has reinforced Acheson's view in observing that "the Soviet Union always tries to get something for nothing and it is ready for a quid pro quo only when its opponent is equally stubborn and persevering." This line of argument suggests that although the Soviets and Chinese have quite often appeared to commit themselves unalterably at the opening of a negotiation to a set of exorbitant, non-negotiable demands, they have proven willing to make essential compromises—but only when it became clear they could not force an acceptance of their positions. Thus, the "greater propensity [of the Soviets] to negotiate seriously on disarmament" than the Americans, as discussed earlier, may be interpreted in this view to be a factor of the timing of concessions coupled with the extreme initial positions of the Soviets. As Jensen (1963: 529-530) suggests, the Americans seemed to be more prepared to compromise in the early stages of the negotiations, but finding the Soviets unwilling to reciprocate, became disillusioned and ready to terminate the discussions; at this point, the Soviets, presumably desirous of continuing the debate, and having maintained throughout a rigid and extreme position, would make a variety of broad and unexpected concessions. The tenor of this interpretation, therefore, is that communist compromise can only be induced when western negotiators adopt a posture of severe intransigence.

Upon examination, it once again becomes clear that there are various perspectives by which to view and explain these stylistic negotiating techniques. Nevertheless, however one chooses to interpret communist negotiating behavior, and whatever determinants one selects to account for their frequent diplomatic intransigence, the evidence suggests that such inflexibility represents a negotiating strategy adaptable to compromise and the achievement of mutual advantage. Western expectations of communist inflexibility, therefore, would seem to be more useful if tempered with expectations of eventual communist accommodation—where such accommodation is recognized as serving communist interests. In short, communist negotiating practice, though characterized by a severe adherence to seemingly unyielding positions, may be expected to reflect the typical adjustive methods employed by any state which seeks a maximization of its desired objectives.

## THE HOSTILE RHETORIC OF COMMUNIST DIPLOMACY

Western negotiations with the Soviets and Chinese, as reported by many observers, have been frequently marked by the explicit expression of communist hostility, reflected in a broad variety of severe pressure tactics, unanticipated gambits, and seemingly inexplicable changes in mood and tempo, all of which have impaired seriously the reaching of accord on conflictual issues. A seemingly fundamental element of these "adversary proceedings" has been an extensive reliance by the communists on an array of tactical bluffs and warnings which often are escalated into bellicose threats and menacing ultimatums. Furthermore, this antagonistic approach generally is said (K. J. Holsti, 1972: 202) to be accompanied by abusive and intemperate, propaganda-oriented language—a diplomatic rhetoric commonly compossed of outrageous "epithets, crudities, and vulgarisms." As Acheson (1961: 90-91) observes, it seems as if communist negotiators have attended "a school of dialectics, where naturally coarse manners were made intentionally offensive, and where the students were trained in a technique of intellectual deviousness designed to frustrate any discussion." Thus, in their contentious approach to negotiations, the Soviets and Chinese are again charged (Kertesz, 1959: 169) with having abandoned the procedural rules of traditional diplomacy by employing "invective, provocations, and other harsh methods [which] exclude the possibility of serene and constructive diplomatic intercourse." These charges, like others discussed in the preceding sections, represent a serious indictment of communist diplomatic practice and warrant further analysis.

Aggressive postures in diplomatic negotiations are hardly unique to the communists, for bluffs, warnings, threats, and ultimatums have long represented common methods for attempting to pressure and demoralize one's opponent and thereby induce acquiescence to one's demands. The issue, then, is not whether the communists employ such tactics, for it would indeed be surprising if they did not; rather, the proper question which should be raised here involves whether or not the communists are more prone than western negotiators to the use of such combative diplomatic measures. Unfortunately, in the absence of any useful comparative quantitative studies dealing with this subject, the charges against the Soviets and Chinese in this case appear to be subjective judgemental issues that can be neither verified nor refuted with any degree of objective certainty. Of course, the common perceptual belief that such is indeed the case undoubtedly has played a major role in structuring the attitudes and approaches developed by many western diplomats for use in their negotiations with the communist states; and, as noted previously, such perceptions may severely exacerbate already strained diplomatic relations.

## Vilification of the Adversary

A more readily examined dimension of communist diplomatic belligerency, however, involves their apparent unique oratorical techniques, for here they seem to have clearly distinguished themselves in their constant denigration of both the positions and the personal character of their western negotiating opponents. The pejorative attacks on "ruling circles" which control western politics and are engaged continually in hatching "counter-revolutionary," "reactionary," and "imperialist" plots against the socialist countries, though typical of communist rhetoric, do not even begin to reflect the extreme nature of their diplomatic language. For example, one especially interesting feature of their style of discussion involves the frequent refusal of either the Soviets or the Chinese to use correct titles when referring to western diplomatic representatives and their governments. Instead of following standard diplomatic amenities, communist negotiators are reported (Holsti, 1972: 202) to have repeatedly employed, both publicly and privately, "such terms of derision as 'fascists,' 'warmongers,' 'lackeys,' 'stooges,' or, in the case of the communist Chinese characterization of several statesmen attempting to act as mediators to the Vietnamese War, as 'freaks,' 'monsters,' and 'nitwits.'"

Illustrations of such deprecative language abound in the memoir literature, but seem to be far more characteristic of recent Chinese than Soviet practice, with Soviet moderation possibly reflective of changing leadership styles as previously noted. Perhaps the most dramatic examples of Chinese offensiveness occurred at Panmunjom. Instead of speaking of the governments of the Republic of Korea or the Republic of China, the Communist Chinese and Korean delegations consistently spoke of the "running dogs" of "the murderer Rhee" and the U.S. "puppet on Formosa" (Vatcher, 1958: 38). Admiral Joy (1955: 16), the senior United Nations delegate at the armistice talks, reports that on one occasion during the discussions a note was exchanged between North Korean delegates which, in Korean characters large enough to be read by the non-communist representatives, proclaimed: "These imperialist errand boys are lower than dogs in a morgue." Joy states that this was "the ultimate Korean insult." In a similar show of disregard for diplomatic courtesy, Huang Hua, the senior Chinese representative at Panmunjom (and currently the Chinese Ambassador to the United Nations) repeatedly referred to American Ambassador Arthur H. Dean (1966b: 54) as "a capitalist crook, rapist, thief, robber of widows, stealer of pennies from the eyes of the dead, [and] mongrel of uncertain origin." At one point after repeatedly charging South Korean President Rhee, President Eisenhower, and Secretary Dulles of the deliberate murder of Koreans and Chinese, Huang added that Dean "was a murderer lying in the gutter with filthy garbage, wallowing in the filth of a ram—that there was a saying in Chinese that a man was known by the company he keeps, and that . . . [Dean's] South Korean companions were execrable, filthy, bloody, etc."

Young experienced comparable abusiveness during his negotiations with the Chinese in Warsaw. In his detailed account of the "Ambassadorial Talks," he reports (1968: 146) that the Chinese diplomatic vocabulary would include any or all of the following words to attack the American negotiating positions:

absurd, audacious, fantastic, ridiculous, deceitful, dishonest, distorted, shameful, insincere, intolerable, invidious, impertinent, mendacious, malicious, rapacious, slanderous, preposterous, lecherous, scandalous, vicious, stupid, nonsensical, treacherous, perfidious, etc., through the thesaurus.

Even the most serious American proposals, Young states, were promptly dismissed by the Chinese "as a 'trick,' 'conspiracy,' 'fraud,' 'swindle,' and 'sham.'" Obviously, the negotiating atmosphere created by such acrimonious language would not seem very conducive to conflict resolution.

## Perceptions and Propaganda

The use of such reviling and vituperative language, characterized by frequent accusations of "treacherous designs," "evil intentions," "perfidious actions," and a "connivance to violate agreements," may well represent the actual Soviet and Chinese perceptions of their western adversaries. At the very least, this aspect of communist negotiating style seems calculated to project an image of their perceptions (Jervis, 1970: 10). However, as with other communist methods, the projection of such images may be intentionally deceptive; the objective here would be to try to make one's opponent believe that he is truly perceived in this manner. For the western diplomat, such an image of himself and his nation, regardless of its merit, might conceivably prove personally intolerable; and forced on the defensive, such western diplomats might thereby be induced into making various concessions that otherwise would not be forthcoming. On the other hand, such behavior might so antagonize one's opponent that he might well strengthen his will to persevere, as was the west's response to heightened Soviet verbal attacks in the post-World War II period. However, such overt rhetorical hostility has been insightfully interpreted as having an inherently pragmatic utility, that of disguising one's own weaknesses in dealing with a more powerful opponent. Arguing that "it pays to be rude," Nathan Leites (1953: 37) suggests that this was precisely the Soviets objective in their verbal offensive against their former allies, as the U.S.S.R. sought to conceal the emergent assymetry of East-West capabilities. Leites' analysis suggests that when such offensive behavior is encountered, it may in large part be designed to heighten an opponent's estimate of the communists real power and determination; and if the adversary is in retreat, it may prompt him "to relinquish positions which he had not quite decided to give up."

In a related fashion, the constant reiteration of communist insults, accompanied by such other commonly reported practices as playing up alleged grievances, repeating accusations of bad faith, and walking temporarily out of diplomatic conferences, may all represent orchestrated attempts to create a maximum propaganda and emotional impact. Such an interpretation of these features of communist diplomatic behavior would seem to be especially appropriate for understanding negotiations in which "side effects" are important objectives—perhaps even more important than achieving a resolution of conflict. Thus, one encounters the frequently experienced phenomena of negotiations in which "the basic appeals are made to the galleries of world public opinion rather than across the table to the opposition" (Jensen, 1963: 522).

Much of the earlier discussion of the communist techniques of prolonging negotiating sessions through seemingly endless reiterations of inflexible positions, and their interminable haggling over minor and often merely procedural points, also seems to reflect a similar propaganda dimension. Though such tactics have frustrated scores of western diplomats and have played a large part in causing "negative outcomes" in negotiations with the Soviets and Chinese, these stylistic measures must be viewed by the communists as having some functional utility, for how else might one account for their continued practice? Committed to the propagation of their particularistic views of "objective reality," "historical determinism," and so on, negotiations with the west would appear to provide a useful forum for the dissemination of their ideological *weltanschauung*. That such is indeed the case is supported by their explicit recognition of the prominent role of propaganda in international negotiations, as revealed in the following passage (cited in U.S. Senate, 1969b: 80-81) from the Soviet *Diplomatic Dictionary*:

> The unmasking of the aggressive plans and actions of imperalists is one of the important methods of socialist diplomacy, assisting it to mobilize democratic public opinion and popular masses throughout the entire world against the aggressive policy of imperialist governments.

Examination of communist diplomatic rhetoric, therefore, suggests that although the extreme demands and extraordinary proposals of the Soviets and Chinese may not represent their actual expectations, they may serve the dual roles of spreading their message while simultaneously establishing bargaining positions from which it may prove possible to evoke important western concessions. Whether the communists are successful in such cases may depend as much on the personality of the western negotiator as on the substance of the negotiation. While most diplomats may readily recognize that certain Soviet and Chinese demands may be based on unfounded claims and false accusations, they nevertheless must find some way of dealing with such issues. Moreover, though it may be true that "an oft-repeated lie cannot become the truth," it should be recognized that a constant reiteration of the same charges and an unremitting repetition of claims for the redressing of alleged evils—past and present—may eventually prove convincing, at least in the sense "that a view heard often enough must contain a grain of truth and should be given proper attention" (Kulski, 1964: 594). By way of illustration, the Soviet and Chinese governments reportedly "always assume the posture of an injured party which has the right to redress," but is hampered by adversaries dedicated to preserving the established order; and, as Kulski (1964: 595) suggests, although their initial claim "might be spurious or greatly inflated . . ., the constant hammering on its reasonableness and justice might eventually convince the opponent that the existing status quo is truly abnormal and should become the topic of negotiation."

The linkage of communist propaganda with their rejection of the international status quo has prompted some western analysts (such as Kissinger, 1957: 337) to conclude that it is futile to try to negotiate with the communists "by 'ordinary' diplomatic methods." It has been argued that as representatives of states dedicated to revolutionary change in the international system, the Soviets and Chinese are compelled to reject the diplomatic procedures and structural processes which, in their view, have been developed specifically to constrain such change. Thus, unprepared to "allow the international order to remain undisturbed," the communist states emerge as "unreasonable and pugnacious," as "demanding and bellicose," precisely because "they are trying to break the rules which delegate them to second place when they seek to be first" (Organski, 1968: 387).

Presuming a commitment by the Soviets and Chinese to a fundamental alteration of the international system, it seems understandable that they would be inclined in their diplomatic rhetoric to reduce all arguments to the basic proposition that their views are the only correct ones and represent the true desires of all repressed peoples in the world. In their ideological perspective, therefore, the complexities of international conflicts may be reduced to simplistic black and white issues which thoroughly discredit the position of one's adversary. In his reported reply (Vatcher, 1958: 212) to a United Nations proposal at Panmunjom, General Nam II, the North Korean senior delegate, amply illustrated this technique: "[Your proposal] is completely groundless and unworthy of consideration and cannot be considered. On the other hand . . ., our proposal is one which is recognized by the whole world and one which is just, reasonable, realistic and practicable." Spanier and Nogee (1962: 49) observed a related rhetorical process in conjunction with Soviet behavior in their extensive disarmament negotiations with the west. Rejecting all western-proposed systems of inspection and control, the Soviets claimed commitment to a policy of "complete and general disarmament," a phrase they "repeated over and over again as if, in a trance, they were invoking a magic formula to heal all the earth's wounds." Thus, if the western powers "accepted the Soviet scheme, they were obviously, like the Russians and their friends, for peace; if they objected to the plan, they were equally obviously 'warmongers' and against peace—and quite probably, also against virtue, motherhood and holidays for school children."

Chinese communist statements during the "Ambassadorial Talks" in Geneva and Warsaw are reported to have been characterized by comparable propaganda techniques, leading Ambassador Young (1968: 370) to conclude that the Chinese negotiating style was "designed not to facilitate the task of his opposite numbers but to harass and exasperate them as much as possible." Young's summary comments on this stylistic aspect of Chinese negotiating behavior are characteristic of the literature. In his view, the Chinese negotiator:

> will try to prove that the Americans are deceitful and unreliable by not accepting Peking's proposition without question. If the Americans were "sincere," they would only have to sign on the dotted line and ask no questions. Badgering the Americans constantly, the Chinese negotiator tries to put them on the defensive in order to make them reply that they are indeed sincere and will, therefore, come to an agreement.

## Harassment and Procedural Conflict

It is in the preliminary stages of negotiations with the Soviets and Chinese that the harassment and badgering techniques described above seem to be most prominently displayed. Apart from the propaganda objectives previously discussed, the presentation of grievances, the accusations of misconduct, and the issuance of extreme warnings—all characteristic features of the initial meetings—seem to be directly related to the issues of framing the conference agenda and establishing the procedural rules to be followed during the negotiations. As many analysts have reported, the matter of scheduling the order of discussion of substantive issues may well establish the eventual outcome of negotiations with the communists. In one experienced participant's view (Dean, 1966b: 49), "The battle of the agenda is fundamental to communist negotiators because they believe they can humiliate the other side and [either] win or lose a conference in this first battle. . . . Quite often they are correct."

Obviously, these preliminary aspects of international negotiations are of equal concern to western negotiators who have a vested interest in establishing an agenda and procedures favorable to their side; however, most reports portray the Soviets and Chinese as the principal offensive combatants in the "agenda battle," and a variety of objectives may be involved in their contentious struggle. For example, a fairly conventional purpose for attempting to control the format of any negotiation—and one which often results in a serious diplomatic conflict—is the effort by all sides to restrict the agenda to those issues with which they are most directly concerned and for which they believe they have the greater bargaining advantage. Since either side may obtain a superior negotiating position in this manner, such an objective does not seem to be the unique province of the Soviets or Chinese.

A more distinctive objective in the debate over formulating the agenda and related procedures may be to place specific "items at the top of the agenda in order to have a chance to secure an agreement on them before discussing items of greater interest to the other state" (Kulski, 1964: 596). In Ambassador Dean's (1966b: 49) view, the advantage of such a "stacked agenda" generally goes to the communist side, for as his experience attests, "if you once agree to the communist order, you cannot go on to the next item until you have yielded to the communist wishes on the first." This tactic is in direct contrast to the general western tradition of placing less controversial and more readily resolvable issues at the top of the agenda so as to "permit group procedures to develop more fully before critical matters are treated" (Sawyer and Guetzkow, 1965: 473). Schelling (1969: 44-46), for example, has shown how the dynamics of cooperation may often be induced and the overall negotiating process be improved by treating a larger transaction as a series of smaller ones, each one dependent on the successful completion of the preceding ones. According to most western observers, however, the Soviet and Chinese approach most often seems to be designed to insure that the initial transaction is of such importance that its resolution—or non-resolution—determines the outcome of the entire negotiation.

Finally, the effort to control the agenda may be directed at fixing the actual substance of the negotiations: rather than treating the agenda simply as a general list of subjects to be discussed, the purpose may be to phrase the items in such a way as to list specific conclusions which are favorable to one side—a technique frequently attributed to the communists. As an example (Joy, 1955: 19), an agenda item proposed by the United Nations representatives at the Korean Armistice negotiations read simply, "Agreement on a demilitarized zone across Korea." The counterpart communist proposed item, however, read much more specifically, "Establishment of the *38th Parallel* as the military demarcation line between both sides." Although the United Nations delegation was willing in the preliminary meetings to accept the concept of a general demilitarized zone, the specific location and limits of such a zone was felt to be more properly the subjects for substantive negotiations rather than a priori conclusions to be inserted in an agenda format.

Such terminological conflicts in preliminary negotiating sessions have even extended into pointed controversies over the appropriate title for designating a conference, and have had subsequently negative impacts on negotiating outcomes. Jacobson and Stein, for example, in their study of the American-Soviet negotiations to effect a nuclear test ban agreement, report that despite a lengthy initial dispute that resulted in entitling the discussions as "The Conference on the Discontinuance of Nuclear Weapons Tests," the parties continued to disagree on the meaning of the word "discontinuance." In the American view, the word indicated only a "suspension" of testing, whereas the Soviets reportedly argued (Jacobson and Stein, 1966: 116-117) that the term called for a total "cessation." As one analyst (Jervis, 1970: 194) points out, this was not merely a semantic disagreement, for it involved the fundamental issue of whether, as the Soviets claimed, the "discontinuance" meant that the conference was designed to produce a permanent and unconditional halt to atmospheric nuclear testing, rather than a specified suspension period as the Americans contended. In this particular case, of course, both sides seem to share responsibility for the problem; by their very acceptance of the term "discontinuance," they appear to have implicitly "agreed to disagree." When such basic differences in interpretation emerge at the opening of a diplomatic conference, they are likely to persist and produce the various sorts of problems previously noted in conjunction with the discussion of "agreements in principle." Under such conditions, it would be expected that additional misunderstandings, mutual accusations of bad faith, and so forth would arise, contributing further to the difficulty of reaching a viable settlement and adding to the perception of the "other side" as the guilty party.

Just as rhetorical haggling over the formulation of conference agendas may be designed to exert influence over the substantive issues at hand, so too may such wrangling over other procedural matters have similar objectives. Such a situation seems to have occurred, for example, in Geneva in 1951 at the Conference of Foreign Ministers where Soviet insistence on a particular seating arrangement was aimed at providing the East German delegation with formal recognition and international status. Similar dickering over diplomatic seating arrangements, for comparable purposes, occurred at the Geneva Conference on Laos in 1961 involving the seating of the three separate Lao delegations; and of course there was the notable controversy in 1968 at the Vietnam "Peace Talks" in Paris where it took seventy-seven days to agree on the shape of the table (a round one was finally selected) at which the representatives of the Viet Cong, North and South Vietnam, and the United States would be seated. It should be recognized that such procedural issues have been fairly common in international negotiations. It has been reported (Sawyer and Guetzkow, 1965: 472) that during the efforts to end the Thirty Years War in Europe during the seventeenth century, the discussions which resulted in the eventual Peace of Westphalia could not even be begun for some three months, as the delegations debated the problem of the order in which they should enter and be seated in the negotiating chamber. Similarly, Morgenthau (1973: 77) notes that the Potsdam Conference in 1945 could not get underway until Truman, Churchill, and Stalin had achieved some mode of entering the conference room which treated each delegation as equals; they accomplished this by arranging to emerge simultaneously from three separate doors. Numerous other illustrations of such seemingly insignificant procedural matters could be provided to demonstrate the almost universal nature of such problems. However, in most of the historical cases cited in the literature, these procedural issues only involved matters of diplomatic protocol, whereas in the communist cases described above, the principle issue was that of getting the western states to extend diplomatic recognition to delegations representing disputed states or revolutionary groups— quite a different matter. Moreover, in these latter cases, it has generally been the western states (or their allies) which have been most reluctant to modify their positions, as at Paris where the South Vietnamese rather than the communists are reported (Harriman, 1971: 127) to have created the lengthy procedural delay.

Many of the various problems examined thus far—attacks on the personal character of western diplomats, squabbles over conference agendas, and prolonged quarrels over minor and noncritical issues—are often interpreted as communist techniques for insuring negotiating outcomes favorable to their side. However, it is quite possible that the harassment and conflict that these techniques evoke may have other purposes. It is conceivable, for example, that the goal in certain cases may be to deliberately wreck a negotiation the communists did not want to succeed in the first place. It is obviously difficult to determine when such an objective may be operative inasmuch as the Soviets and Chinese would not be likely to make it known; however, at least one case of this sort has been reported (Dean, 1966b: 52). The situation occurred during the Korean post-armistice talks at Panmunjom when United Nations representatives were attempting to achieve an agreement on arrangements for a "political conference" which would be aimed at achieving a true Korean peace settlement—a conference which has yet to take place. Although the communist delegations gave verbal support to such a conference, their militant attitude and constant bickering over the details raised questions as to their real commitment to effecting such an agreement. Western suspicions seemed to be confirmed when members of the Indian contingent of the Neutral Nations Supervisory Committee (which had been appointed to oversee the armistice agreements) reportedly were candidly advised by the Chinese "that they never intended to come to an agreement—that they intended to change their position as soon as an agreement was reached, so that the burden of not bringing a lasting peace in Korea would be on the United States."

## Rejection of Interpersonal Relations

One final point should be examined with regard to the many western reports of harassment and hostility which contribute to the image of the implacable and intransigent communist negotiator. To help induce an atmosphere conducive to more cooperative and less hostile forms of bargaining behavior, western diplomats dealing with the Soviets and Chinese have repeatedly attempted to effect the "professional private contacts and confidential exchanges of views on a personal basis . . . which have led to many fruitful negotiations in the past" among western states (Kertesz, 1959: 149). Most such efforts, unfortunately, have not received acceptance by the communists. Dean (1966b: 47), for example, points out how his attempts proved fruitless at the Korean post-armistice meeting where procedures had been instituted by the Chinese and North Koreans to thoroughly prohibit any fraternization with western representatives. He reports that "no individual could speak personally to anyone on the other side," and "there could be no exchange even of ordinary amenities," since the western delegates were forbidden to ask the communists "over to the U.N. side for a drink, a meal, or a conversation." Dean concludes, "There was no way in which the normal tensions of difficult diplomatic negotiations could be relieved, and no way in which private negotiations or suggestions could be carried out."

Ambassadors Gronouski (1966: 44-46) and Young (1968) in relating their experiences at the Ambassadorial Talks in Warsaw, report similar rejections by the Chinese. Both ambassadors shared a belief in the contributory worth of private meetings and social relations for developing "some kind of personal rapport" which would enable the two sides to better "understand each other and contribute to the progress of the talks." But neither Gronouski nor Young could induce such behavior from the Chinese who remained "to themselves, strictly segregated and uncommunicative" (Young, 1968: 483).

Comparable personal approaches also generally have proven difficult in relations with Soviet diplomats. Former British Ambassador to Moscow, Sir William Hayter, is reported to have claimed (Acheson, 1961: 91) that even with individual Soviets, it was not "possible to establish any kind of lasting or genuine personal relationships;" and with "the real rulers of Russia . . ., it was the same distressing experience of all Ambassadors that these great men had no more to say in private than in public; the same series of gramaphone records was played on every occasion; nothing emerged from these private conversations that could not just as well be gleaned from the pages of Pravda." Many other western diplomats have shared these views. Kennan (1967: 561), for one, has advised westerners against trying "to act chummy with" the Soviets, arguing that "this only embarasses them individually and deepens their suspicions, for they "abhor the thought of appearing before their own people as one who has become buddies with a foreigner." Similarly, Harriman (1975: 3-4) who has had as much experience as any westerner in negotiating with the communists, has recently argued that western diplomats "cannot be friendly with the communists" because of fundamental differences in "their basic loyalties and conceptions." Pointing to ideological and historical barriers, Harriman claims that "there is a certain point you can't go beyond because they are taught to believe that man is destined to live by the communist ideology, and that we, the imperialist aggressors, are blocking it." Thus, he concludes, "you can talk about a man's religion up to a point and you can't go beyond it."

Curiously, however, Ambassador Dean (1966a: 35), who experienced such difficulty in this area in his dealings with the Chinese, found a somewhat different situation in his meetings with the Soviets at Geneva in 1961-1963 during the disarmament and nuclear test ban negotiations. In the formal sessions, he encountered the common forms of harrassment and intransigence which have been discussed earlier. However, Dean found the Soviets apparently quite willing to engage in "private, off-the-record meetings" which proved "cordial and much more reasonable" than the "time-consuming, repetitious, and . . . rather banal, long-winded, and stereotyped exchanges at the official sessions." In fact, contrary to what Hayter, Kennan, Harriman, and others report, Dean claims that it was possible in such private working sessions with the Soviets, "to talk dispassionately and intelligently about a number of controversial topics, to explore each other's meanings and interpretations, and to get down to [the] detailed drafting" of agreements. Similarly, Newhouse (1973: 212-213) reports that during the latter phases of the American-Soviet SALT I negotiations, "informal contact between the delegations increased steadily," including "tete-a-tete lunches and dinners" and many private meetings among the principals. Newhouse explains this behavior in terms of the "vested interests" that both delegations had developed "in making some progress," and that, "in a broad sense, they were becoming accomplices, seeking to narrow differences between their governments, looking for bargaining room." These reports reflect some of the variations western negotiators have observed in communist diplomatic behavior; and whether such variations are the result of diverse personality styles, differing issue content, discriminate negotiating objectives, or some combination of these and still other variables, they illustrate further the fallacy of presuming a fixed, fundamental, and unalterable pattern of communist negotiating practice.

Finally, any examination of the extraordinary rhetorical abuse and hostile tactics which are said to characterize Soviet and Chinese negotiating style must also take into account the various historical, ideological, and perceptual factors described earlier. As has been demonstrated, unsatisfactory historical experiences, conflicting value systems, and mutual perceptions of one's negotiating counterpart as a "treacherous enemy" seem to be significant factors in the contentious behaviors described herein. From a psychological point of view, it may be that the communists simply find it extremely difficult to continue to view themselves as dedicated revolutionaries while at the same time being cordial and polite to the "capitalist reactionaries" in the enemy camp. Moreover, if such aggressive stances seem to prove functional in eliciting concessions from their western adversaries, the communists may believe—and perhaps correctly—that these aspects of their diplomatic style are more effective than if they were to adopt less conflictual methods. Of course, for western diplomats, Soviet and Chinese harassment and belligerency only seem to reinforce their inordinately negative appraisal of communist negotiators and to further aggravate already strained relations. The problems here are real and substantial; and although some limited changes seem to have occurred, particularly with respect to an apparent growing communist willingness to participate in private and constructive discussions with western negotiators, the overall prospects for achieving the fundamental alterations in the perspectives of all sides, so necessary for mutual accommodation and effective resolution of conflict, do not appear very promising.

## CONCLUSION

Although this study has expressly attempted to avoid methodological involvement in the problematic and questionable task of developing a generalized model of communist negotiating behavior, such a model—or at least a commonly perceived model—seems to emerge from a survey of the diplomatic and analytical literature on the subject. In the view of most western observers, the Soviets and Chinese have indeed adopted fairly comparable obstructionist negotiating techniques for dealing with the west—techniques which most analysts seem to agree reflect a specific disregard, if not deliberate rejection, of many of the fundamental methods of traditional western diplomacy. Most importantly, the stereotypical model which is projected is an extraordinarily negative one in which communist negotiators are portrayed as deceptive and duplicitous, secretive and suspicious, inflexible and implacable, contentious and contemptuous. Soviet and Chinese negotiating behavior, it is usually argued, reflects an ideological discipline and nationalistic orientation which produces an unswerving belief in the absolute faultlessness of the communist position and inevitable victory for the communist side. Thus, most observers conclude that these factors, coupled with important historical and cultural considerations, account for the Soviet and Chinese treatment of negotiations with the west as antagonistic proceedings between dedicated mortal enemies—adversary engagements more suitable for purposes of communist propaganda, revolutionary agitation, and national intimidation than as means for communication, collective bargaining, and the mutual adjustment of differences.

There is certainly considerable evidence supportive of such views, as indicated throughout this study. At the same time, however, there have been several cases, similarly noted, wherein Soviet and Chinese negotiating behavior departed significantly from the stringent model outlined above, and resulted in compromised settlements providing some degree of mutual satisfaction. Apart from the examples cited from the Cold War era, it seems apparent that conditions for such accommodation prevailed and were cultivated by both sides in the diplomatic proceedings which led to the notable and varied American-Soviet arms control agreements of the past decade, as well as to the negotiated accommodation reached in recent years between the United States and the People's Republic of China.[28] Moreover, the primacy so often ascribed to ideological, cultural, and psychological variables, appears in these cases to have been overshadowed by critical pragmatic considerations.

Other deviations from the obstructionist model have been identified. Analysis suggests, for example, that although communist diplomats may be severely constrained in their activities by governmental direction, they nevertheless possess a greater measure of authority and flexibility than is usually presumed. This seems to be particularly evident in those cases where their governments have proven willing, however reluctantly, to engage in the adjustive bargaining believed necessary to attain desired policy objectives. Further, although there is far less information available for examining the Chinese case than for that of the Soviets, there do appear to be several dissimilarities in various aspects of their respective diplomatic behavior, notably in their relative use of deception, in their comparative employment of bombastic rhetoric, and in their willingness to engage in interpersonal relationships with western diplomats. Finally, western accounts tend to impute a "unitary, rational actor" role to the behaviors of each country, failing to recognize the presence of bureaucratic and organizational dynamics which may involve internal policy-making disputes within the Soviet and Chinese governments and result in important variations in their respective patterns of negotiation. In short, upon subjection to critical analysis, the systemic regularities commonly attributed to communist negotiating behavior tend to lose their constancy and uniformity, and serious questions are raised as to the appropriateness as well as the utility of generalized conceptualizations.

Much of the difficulty obviously is analytic in nature. As was demonstrated in our discussion of alleged deceptive practices, questions of ambiguity and incertitude plague the study of communist diplomacy. Forced to deal with such uncertainty, western negotiators generally have appeared reluctant to grant the Soviets or Chinese the benefit of doubt; rather, by relying heavily on past experiences and the judgements of others, they have tended to reinforce prevailing denigrative opinions of communist diplomatic conduct, while at the same time perpetuating a self-righteous view of their own behavior. Essentially, the issue centers on perceptual biases and preconceived expectations which often impair objective appraisals and promote disparaging assessments. This problem is particularly acute in those cases where adjustive and accommodative communist behavior—when it does occur—is viewed with suspicion and skepticism, and is attributed to ulterior, potentially threatening motivations. Thus, where flexibility replaces rigidity, and cooperation supplants nonaccommodation, such situations, if not dismissed as aberrations, are frequently viewed as tactical ploys to achieve communist objectives which will prove ultimately disadvantageous to the west.

All of these summary observations suggest, therefore, that a general western reevaluation of communist negotiating behavior is in order. Although several studies have addressed the issue of developing appropriate strategies for western negotiations with the Soviets and Chinese, they often have been based on elements of the negatively oriented model of communist diplomacy described here.[29] Such prescriptions, therefore, may not be very suitable or advisable, particularly when they fail to account for negotiating situations in which all sides share a mutual interest in achieving an effective resolution of conflict. An important exception here, however, would be the work of Iklé (1964; and U.S. Senate, 1970) whose various recommendations to avoid treating communist negotiating positions as immutable, to halt the prenegotiating practice of discarding so-called "unacceptable" proposals, and to follow policies of patient perseverance as well as accommodative flexibility appear quite valid in view of the present findings. Yet, apart from such generalized suggestions, the western negotiator must have the talent and the training necessary to permit him to implement strategies suitable to specific negotiating situations where the outcome may be dependent on a broad variety of unspecific conditions; and in terms of the successful resolution of conflict, he must possess the ability to discern and promote those conditions which are compatible with such resolution.

In view of such requirements, rigorous analytical attention needs to be given to the admittedly difficult problem of systematically identifying and comparing the various conditions which have prevailed on those occasions in which communist negotiators have employed fairly conciliatory, nonobstructionist patterns of diplomatic negotiation. Although in certain cases the pertinent conditions may prove so situationally determined that generalizations may only be suggestive, it seems likely that detailed analyses of specific instances of accommodative communist negotiations may prove fruitful in identifying some important behavioral regularities. At the very least, such methodic appraisals should prove more objective and illuminating than many of the general studies which are currently available. In addition to the contributions which might result from such future analyses, systematic observations by participant diplomats, well-schooled in the multidimensional aspects of behavioral interaction might prove a significant means of achieving more appropriate insights into Soviet and Chinese negotiating behavior. Further, such efforts might have the salutary effect of helping to remedy many of the deficiences previously noted (Macomber, 1975: 46) in the present preparation of western diplomatic representatives.

# NOTES

1. The traditional western approach to negotiation is well summarized by K. J. Holsti (1972: 200-202) who has outlined several Anglo-American assumptions regarding appropriate types and suitable practices of diplomatic conduct. These are said to include the following: confidence that "any agreement can be reached through compromise;" trust that "expressions of good will toward the opponent, as well as frankness and candor in discussions, will produce an atmosphere conducive to compromise;" preference for "compromise and subsequent reconciliation" as opposed to "total victory and vindictiveness;" belief in negotiation as a means of achieving agreement rather than of prolonging conflict; and emphasis on a "willingness to compromise, desire for fairness, sincerity, honesty, good will, and cooperation." These statements obviously represent an idealized version of western norms; yet, they typify the conventional western self-image. Although Holsti admits to western deviations, in company with other observers (such as Aspaturian, 1963: 46-47) he dismisses such variances as aberrations which appear to be either "individual blunders, or ploys useful for very particular bargaining situations," or as "no more than an expression of extreme frustration with the bargaining practices of opponents." Western perceptions of communist deviations are much more critical, as will be demonstrated.

2. It is quite likely that Kissinger's extensive practical diplomatic experience since 1969 has altered his earlier harsh appraisal of Soviet negotiating behavior, an appraisal drawn largely on the basis of the Cold War period. Indeed, much of what appears in the present study represents western attitudes and perceptions formulated during that time of overt East-West political hostility; and it is recognized that if the writers of that period, many of whom seem to have drawn heavily on the observations of each other, were to reevaluate their work in view of contemporary political conditions, many might choose to revise their views. Nevertheless, earlier western assessments—however questionable in terms of their current validity—have tended to be perpetuated; and several recent observers have continued to view communist diplomacy as obstructionist—as a zero-sum approach to conflict which rejects traditional western principles of accommodative negotiation. Nowhere is this image more apparent than in the 1972 Senate testimony of William R. Van Cleave (1972a: 200). Van Cleave, advisor on the U.S. SALT delegation, argued that the Soviet Union, unlike the United States, did not see the SALT negotiations as "a cooperative process—as one in which both sides perceived the objectives and urgencies similarly" in search of a "common goal of strategic stability;" rather, in words strikingly reminiscent of Kissinger's early views, Van Cleave concluded, "The Soviet Union . . . seems clearly to have regarded SALT as another competitive endeavor, where the objective is unilateral advantage and where one can gain at the expense of the other."

3. The closest approach to such a study is found in the rather polemical and undocumented monograph of Steibel (1972).

4. Macomber adds: "It is particularly unfortunate that the systematic development of this core skill [that is, negotiation] is one of diplomacy's most neglected areas."

5. Holsti (1972: 206-207), for example, reports "there is considerable evidence that . . . Soviet diplomatic style has been changing. . . . Propaganda, stalling, threats, and an inflexible assumption of the correctness of their own bargaining positions remain integral aspects of typical Soviet and Chinese diplomatic behavior, but the vulgarity, bluster and rigidity of Molotov or Vyshinsky are for the most part absent in the diplomacy of their successors."

6. Kenneth Young (1968: 18-19) has noted a "curiously paradoxical feature" of the U.S.–China Ambassadorial Talks conducted in Geneva and Warsaw from 1953 through 1967:

> At first each government perhaps unwittingly tended to use the customary concept and style of negotiating of the other. Chou En-lai and Ambassador Wang Ping-an in the initial period seem now to have followed the pragmatic and relative Western style of mutual bargaining in "good faith" for a commonly transacted result advantageous in varying degrees to both parties. In contrast, the Americans then seem to have negotiated more in the fashion of China's traditional style of absolutistic, unilateral insistence on the other party's acceptance of general principles and abstract criteria of an ethical or moral nature unobjectionable in and of themselves but far above the give and take process of litigating differences and transacting compromises. In the reversal since 1960 each government has reverted to its own customary style of negotiating which evolved into a composite style of adversary negotiations.

7. During World War II, for example, with the Soviet Union allied militarily with the United States against the Axis powers, American representatives in Moscow reported considerable difficulty in dealing with such apparently nonconflictual issues as improvements in military coordination, facilitation of lend-lease deliveries, and increased technical and cultural exchanges. On these points, see Deane (1947); Standley and Ageton (1955); Hazard (1951); and Herring (1973). Similarly, Frolic (1976), while serving in the People's Republic of China in 1975 as a Canadian diplomat in charge of negotiating and administering "all educational, cultural, scientific, technical, medical, and sports exchanges" between the two countries, reports that despite the fact that his negotiations with the Chinese involved nonconflictual and relatively unimportant issues, the Chinese representatives proved "tough, resourceful, and above all, inflexible."

8. Definitional descriptions of negotiation and diplomacy emphasize the function of conflict resolution. Lall (1966: 5) speaks of international negotiations as "the process of consideration of an international dispute or situation by peaceful means, other than judicial or arbitral processes, with a view to promoting or reaching among the parties concerned or interested some understanding, amelioration, adjustment, or settlement of the dispute or situation." Similarly, Iklé (1964: 3-4) defines negotiation "as a process in which explicit proposals are put forward ostensibly for the purpose of reaching agreement on an exchange or on the realization of a common interest where conflicting interests are present." Finally, in The International Relations Dictionary (Plano and Olton, 1969: 218), negotiation is described as "a diplomatic technique for the peaceful settlement of differences and the advancement of national interests . . . accomplished by compromises and accommodations."

9. Also, in Aspaturian's (1963: 42-43) pointedly biased attack on Soviet diplomacy, he castigates Premier Khrushchev for his deceptive direction of the Cuban affair, characterizing him as "an experienced and successful political adventurer skilled in the arcane arts of intrigue and machination, simulation and dissimulation, simple deception as well as refined duplicity," and who, "in his abysmal lack of grace and refinement and in his elephantine nimbleness" is "more a caricature than a model of Machiavelli's ideal prince"—resembling "more a corpulent confederate of the Sicilian Mafia than a lean and lecherous Florentine Condottiere."

10. The meetings were formally entitled "Conference of Experts to Study the Possibility of Detecting Violations of a Possible Agreement on Suspension of Nuclear Tests."

11. An independent analyst, Colin S. Gray (1975), arrived at a similar conclusion. Although he believed there was no evidence to prove that the Soviets had violated any legal requirements of the SALT I agreements, he suggested that they seem to have severely "affronted its spirit—as imputed by Americans," a further example of the importance of perceptual and cognitive considerations.

12. The report of the Soviet admission followed shortly after the violation was revealed unofficially in an American periodical (Aviation Week and Space Technology, 1976) which has been severely critical of American responses to reports of Soviet arms violations.

13. The agreement was signed on September 10, 1955, and is reproduced in Young (1968: 412-413). See Young's discussion of the issue, and also the treatment by Ekvall (1960: 88-102).

14. This last prisoner was John Downey, who, President Nixon admitted, was an American CIA agent (Newsweek, 1973b). Downey reportedly was captured in 1952 when the Chinese shot down an aircraft engaged in a supply mission for Chinese Nationalist operatives on the mainland (Newsweek, 1973a).

15. Former Secretary of State George C. Marshall's reported comments on this matter are instructive. Marshall is said (Rusk, 1960: 362) to have advised a colleague, "Don't ask me to agree in principle; that just means that we haven't agreed yet."

16. For a comprehensive survey of the literature on this subject, see Druckman (1973).

17. The statements attributed to these former foreign service officers are all reported anonymously. See also Craig (1962: 365-366).

18. Harriman (1971: 196) provides an insightful view of these features in his recounting of a story told to him by Alexis Tolstoy, a distant relative of the renowned Leo Tolstoy, and himself a writer of historical novels. The tale involved a Russian peasant who "had put up a traveler for the night. The peasant had shared with his guest his loaf of bread and his last bottle of vodka, and they got drunk together. The next morning, the peasant woke up first. He thought he had been taken in and so he cut the traveler's throat and took his money." Commenting on this story, Harriman points out that Tolstoy related the tale not only "to illustrate the volative temperament of Russian character but also to show the Russian peasants' suspicion of any stranger, not only foreigners."

19. As observed in note 2, one should recognize that this judgement represents Aspaturian's earlier assessment and may not necessarily coincide with his present views.

20. Somewhat chauvinistically, the "petty chicanery of the U-2 affair and the pitiful dissembling of the Bay of Pigs fiasco" by the American government are dismissed by Aspaturian as "ordinary vices of conventional displomacy . . . , *personal rather than structural* in character and . . . *fundamentally distinct* from Soviet exercises in diplomatic perfidy" (pages 46-47, emphasis added). This view of diplomatic deception as institutionalized in communist systems, as opposed ot its idiosyncratic use by the west, is characteristic of the literature on the subject.

21. Interestingly, Lenin claimed this statement originated in "an English proverb."

22. Iklé (U.S. Senate, 1970: 9) has also commented at length on this general subject, stating that "during the formulation of the United States negotiating position within the State Department and in interagency groups in Washington, it happens often that a possible American proposal or a Western demand is voted down as being 'unacceptable' to the Communist side." Yet, as he observes, "by classifying certain proposals as 'unacceptable' to the opponent, our negotiators and policy-planners in fact make them so," and thereby, as he correctly concludes, deny the United States the important "possibility of modifying a Communist position."

23. The incident which gave rise to Harriman's advice involved negotiations with the Soviets toward the end of World War II regarding the delivery of and payment for war surplus property at the end of the hostilities. Acheson, frustrated in his efforts to reach some agreement, applied Harriman's advice; although the negotiations "got nowhere," the interminably protracted discussions were at least concluded, a result, in Acheson's view, "of which there had seemed to be no possibility before."

24. In one of his many interesting personal reflections, Mosely (1960: 24-25) relates how, by "speaking their language," he was able to turn the Soviets' own fear of failure to his personal advantage during the 1944 London discussions involving the terms of a Bulgarian armistice. Mosely suggested he might be officially "punished" by American authorities if he failed to get the Soviet delegation to reverse itself and agree to the payment by Bulgaria of war reparations to Greece. The ploy worked, as the apparently understanding and sympathetic Soviet representatives approved Mosely's plan. Of course, Mosely admits that Bulgaria, then under Soviet control, provided reparations to Greece which reportedly amounted to only "one broken-down wagon and two slat-ribbed cows!" Incidentally, this episode represents another example of western perceptions of Soviet noncompliance with the expectations of an "agreement in principle;" it also illustrates western use of a "strategy of deception."

25. One should not overlook the potential influence that may be exerted by communist diplomatic representatives in effecting such govermental decisions on major positional changes. Through their official reports on the progress—or lack thereof—in a given negotiating situation, communist diplomats may play a significant role here by recommending specific accommodative techniques to achieve their government's desired objectives. Unfortunately, the importance attached to such a role must remain speculative given the classified nature of their governmental communications.

26. Mosely (1960: 32) makes the notable point, and one that has been widely cited in the analytical literature, that the word "compromise" is not native to the Soviet Russian vocabulary and "carries with it no favorable empathy. It is habitually used only in combination with the adjective 'putrid.'"

27. Note the contrast between Stalin's view and that expressed by Khrushchev (U.S. Department of State, 1959: 307) discussed previously regarding the so-called "huckster's approach" to diplomacy.

28. Given the widespread perception of Soviet reluctance to enter into diplomatic commitments with the west, it is illuminating to tally the arms control agreements involving the Soviet Union and the United States. These encompass commitments to prohibit weaponry in the Antarctic (1959), outer space (1967), and the seabed (1971), as well as agreements establishing a direct communications ("hotline") system between Washington and Moscow (1963 and 1971), a limited nuclear test-ban (1963), a nuclear non-proliferation treaty (1968), a nuclear accidents agree-

ment (1971), a biological and toxin weapons convention (1972), and, of course, the SALT agreements (1972).

29. The works of Dean (1966a), Kertesz (1959) Steibel (1972), Young (1968). and several of the U.S. Senate publications cited herein (for example, 1959, 1969a, 1969b, 1970, and 1972b) are typical of this genre.

# REFERENCES

ACHESON, D. (1969) Present at the Creation: My Years in the State Department. New York: Norton.

––– (1961) Sketches From Life of Men I Have Known. New York: Harper.

ALLISON, G. T. (1971) Essence of Decision: Explaining the Cuban Missile Crisis. Boston: Little, Brown.

ALLPORT, F. (1955) Theories of Perception and the Concept of Structure. New York: Wiley.

ASPATURIAN, V. V. (1963) "Dialectics and duplicity in Soviet diplomacy." J. of Internatl. Affairs 17: 42-60.

Aviation Week and Space Technology (1976) "Newest delta sub pivotal in latest SALT violation," 104: 20-21.

BARTOS, O. J. (1967) "How predictable are negotiations?" J. of Conflict Resolution 11: 481-496.

BAUER, R. A. (1961) "Problems of perception and the relations between the United States and the Soviet Union." J. of Conflict Resolution 5: 223-229.

BOORMAN, H. L. and S. A. BOORMAN (1967) "Strategy and national psychology in China." Annals 370: 143-155.

BUNDY, M. (1949) "The test of Yalta." Foreign Affairs 27: 618-629.

BYRNES, J. F. (1947) Speaking Frankly. New York: Harper.

CAMPBELL, J. C. (1956) "Negotiating with the Soviets: some lessons of the war period." Foreign Affairs 24: 305-319.

CRAIG, G. A. (1962) "Techniques of negotiation," in I. O. Lederer (ed.) Russian Foreign Policy: Essays in Historical Perspective. New Haven: Yale Univ. Press.

DEAN, A. H. (1966a) Test Ban and Disarmament: The Path of Negotiation. New York: Harper & Row.

––– (1966b) "What it's like to negotiate with the Chinese." New York Times Magazine (October 30): 44-45.

DEANE, J. R. (1947) The Strange Alliance: The Story of Our Efforts at Wartime Co-operation with Russia. New York: Viking.

DE CALLIERES, F. (1963) On the Manner of Negotiating with Princes. (trans. by A. F. Whyte) South Bend: Univ. of Notre Dame Press.

DENNETT, R. and J. E. JOHNSON [eds.] (1951) Negotiating with the Russians. Boston: World Peace Foundation.

DE RIVERA, J. H. (1968) The Psychological Dimension of Foreign Policy. Columbus: Merrill.

DEUTSCH, K. W. (1968) The Analysis of International Relations. Englewood Cliffs, N.J.: Prentice-Hall.

DRUCKMAN, D. (1973) Human Factors in International Negotiations: Social-Psychological Aspects of International Conflict. Sage Professional Paper in International Studies, 2, 02-001. Beverly Hills and London: Sage Publications.

EKVALL, R. B. (1960) Faithful Echo. New York: Twayne.

FEDDER, E. H. (1964) "Communication and American-Soviet negotiating behavior." Background 8: 105-120.

FLERON, F. J., Jr. [ed.] (1969) Communist Studies and the Social Sciences: Essays on Methodology and Empirical Theory. Chicago: Rand McNally.

FROLIC, B. M. (1976) "Wide-eyed in Peking: a diplomat's diary." New York Times Magazine (January 11): 16-17.

GILPIN, R. (1962) American Scientists and Nuclear Weapons Policy. Princeton, N.J.: Princeton Univ. Press.

GRAY, C. S. (1975) "SALT I aftermath: have the Soviets been cheating?" Air Force Mag. 58: 28-33.

GRONOUSKI, J. (1966) "When the U.S. negotiates with Peiping—in Warsaw." U.S. News and World Report 61: 44-46.

HARRIMAN, W. A. (1975) "Observations on negotiating." J. of International Affairs 9: 1-6.

––– (1971) America and Russia in a Changing World: A Half Century of Personal Observation. New York: Doubleday.

––– and E. ABEL (1975) Special Envoy to Churchill and Stalin: 1941-1946. New York: Random House.

HAYTER, W. (1961) The Diplomacy of the Great Powers. New York: Macmillan.

HAZARD, J. N. (1951) "Negotiating under lend-lease, 1942-1945," in R. Dennett and J. E. Johnson [eds.] Negotiating with the Russians. Boston: World Peace Foundation.

HERRING, G. C., Jr. (1973) Aid to Russia, 1941-1946. New York: Columbia Univ. Press.

HOFFMAN, E. P. and FLERON, F. J., Jr. (1971) The Conduct of Soviet Foreign Policy. Chicago: Aldine-Atherton.

HOLSTI, K. J. (1972) International Politics: A Framework for Analysis. (sec. ed.) Englewood Cliffs, N.J.: Prentice-Hall.

HOLSTI, O. R. (1962) "The belief system and national images: a case study." J. of Conflict Resolution 6: 244-252.

IKLE, F. C. (1964) How Nations Negotiate. New York: Praeger.

JACOBSON, H. and STEIN, E. (1966) Diplomats, Scientists, and Politicians. Ann Arbor: Univ. of Michigan Press.

JENSEN, L. (1963) "Soviet-American bargaining behavior in the postwar disarmament negotiations." J. of Conflict Resolution 7: 522-541.

JERVIS, R. (1970) The Logic of Images in International Relations. Princeton, N.J.: Princeton Univ. Press.

JOY, C. T. (1955) How Communists Negotiate. New York: Macmillan.

KENNAN, G. F. (1972) Memoirs: 1950-1963. Boston: Little, Brown.

––– (1967) Memoirs: 1925-1950. Boston: Little, Brown.

––– (1964) On Dealing with the Communist World. New York: Harper & Row.

KERTESZ, S. D. (1959) "American and Soviet negotiating behavior," in S. D. Kertesz and M. A. Fitzsimons [eds.] Diplomacy in a Changing World. South Bend: Univ. of Notre Dame Press.

KISSINGER, H. A. (1960) The Necessity for Choice. New York: Harper.

––– (1957) Nuclear Weapons and Foreign Policy. New York: Harper.

KLINEBERG, O. (1964) The Human Dimension in International Relations. New York: Holt, Rinehart & Winston.

KOHLER, F. D. (1970) Understanding the Russians: A Citizen's Primer. New York: Harper & Row.

––– (1958) "Address: May 6, 1958." Dept. of State Bull. 38: 901-910.

KULSKI, W. W. (1964) International Politics in a Revolutionary Age. New York: Lippincott.

LALL, A. (1968) How Communist China Negotiates. New York: Columbia Univ. Press.

––– (1966) Modern International Negotiation: Principles and Practice. New York: Columbia Univ. Press.

LANGER, W. and S. E. GLEASON (1952) The Challenge to Isolation. New York: Harper.

LEITES, N. C. (1953) A Study of Bolshevism. Glencoe: Free Press.

MACHIAVELLI, N. (1952) The Prince. (trans. by L. Ricci; rev. by E.R.P. Vincent) New York: New American Library.

MACOMBER, W. (1975) The Angels' Game: A Handbook of Modern Diplomacy. New York: Stein & Day.

MAO TSE-TUNG (1967) "The question of independence and initiative within the united front (November 5, 1938). Selected Works. (vol. 2) Peking: Foreign Languages Press.

MORGENTHAU, H. J. (1973) Politics Among Nations: The Struggle for Power and Peace. (fifth ed.) New York: Knopf.

MOSELY, P. E. (1960) "Some Soviet techniques of negotiation," in P. E. Mosely (ed.) The Kremlin and World Politics: Studies in Soviet Policy and Action. New York: Vintage.

NEWHOUSE, J. (1973) Cold Dawn: The Story of SALT. New York: Holt, Rinehart & Winston.

Newsweek (1973a) "China: free at last," 81 (March 19): 45.

Newsweek (1973b) "Downey's Odyssey," 81 (March 26): 19-20.

New York Times (1976) May 25, pp. 1, 7.

––– (1975a) December 3, p. 19.

––– (1975b) December 10, p. 12.

––– (1970) October 27, p. 1.

NICOLSON, H. (1964) Diplomacy. (third ed.) New York: Oxford Univ. Press.

NITZE, P. H. (1974) "The strategic balance between hope and skepticism." Foreign Policy 17: 136-156.

ORGANSKI, A.F.K. (1968) World Politics. (sec. ed.) New York: Knopf.

OSBORN, F. (1951) "Negotiating on atomic energy," in R. Dennett and J. E. Johnson (eds.) Negotiating with the Russians. Boston: World Peace Foundation.

OSGOOD, C. E. (1960) "Cognitive dynamics in the conduct of human affairs." Public Opinion Q. 24: 341-375.

Peking Review (1963) "Statement by the spokesman of the Chinese government—a comment on the Soviet government's statement of August 21-September 1, 1963," 6: 16.

PLANO, J. C. and R. OLTON (1969) The International Relations Dictionary. New York: Holt, Rinehart & Winston.

RUSK, D. (1960) "The President." Foreign Affairs 38: 353-369.

SAWYER, J. and H. GUETZKOW (1965) Bargaining and Negotiations in International Behavior and Social-Psychological Analysis. New York: Holt, Rinehart & Winston.

SCHELLING, T. C. (1969) The Strategy of Conflict. London: Oxford Univ. Press.

––– (1966) Arms and Influence. New Haven: Yale Univ. Press.

SMITH, W. B. (1950) My Three Years in Moscow. Philadelphia: Lippincott.

SPANIER, J. W. and J. L. NOGEE (1962) The Politics of Disarmament: A Study in Soviet-American Gamesmanship. New York: Praeger.

STANDLEY, W. H. and A. A. AGETON (1955) Admiral Ambassador to Russia. Chicago: Regnery.

STEIBEL, G. L. (1972) How Can We Negotiate with the Communists? New York: National Strategy Info. Center.

U.S. Department of State (1959) Foreign Ministers Meeting, May-August 1959, Geneva, International Organization and Conference Series, vol. 8. Washington, D.C.: Gov. Print. Office.

U.S. Department of State Bulletin (1963) vol. 48 (February 25). Washington, D.C.: Gov. Print. Office.

U.S. Senate (1973) Hearings before the Permanent Subcommittee on Investigations of the Committee on Government Operations, part 2, with Leopold Labedz, 93d Cong., 1st sess.

––– (1972a) Hearings before the Subcommittee on National Security and International Operations of the Committee on Government Operations, part 7, with William R. Van Cleave, 92d Cong., 2d sess.

––– (1972b) International Negotiation: Some Operational Principles of Soviet Foreign Policy. Prepared by Richard Pipes for the Subcommittee on National Security and International Operations of the Committee on Government Operations, 92d Cong., 2d sess.

––– (1970) International Negotiation: American Shortcomings in Negotiating with Communist Powers. Prepared by Fred C. Iklé for the Subcommittee on National Security and International Operations of the Committee on Government Operations, 91st Cong., 2d sess.

––– (1969a) Peking's Approach to Negotiation: Selected Writings. Prepared for the Subcommittee on National Security and International Operations of the Committee on Government Operations, 91st Cong., 1st sess.

––– (1969b) The Soviet Approach to Negotiation: Selected Writings. Prepared for the Subcommittee on National Security and International Operations of the Committee on Government Operations, 91st Cong., 1st sess.

––– (1959) Study of United States Foreign Policy: Summary of Views of Retired Foreign Service Officers. Prepared for the Committee on Foreign Relations, 86th Cong., 1st sess.

VATCHER, W. H., Jr. (1958) Panmunjom: The Story of the Korean Military Armistice Negotiations. New York: Praeger.

WELCH, W. (1970) American Images of Soviet Foreign Policy. New Haven: Yale Univ. Press.

YOUNG, K. T. (1968) Negotiating with the Chinese Communists: The United States Experience, 1953-1967. New York: McGraw-Hill.

ZARTMAN, I. W. (1975) "Negotiations: theory and reality." J. of Internatl. Affairs 9: 69-77.

*LOUIS J. SAMELSON, professor of Aerospace Studies at Florida Technological University, received his B.A. from San Francisco State College and a Ph.D. in political science from the University of Illinois. A major in the U.S. Air Force, he is the author of the Air Force text on the teaching of American defense policy and civil-military relations, and has published articles on these subjects in Air Force publications. He is presently working on a study of political participation and institutional stability in contemporary China.*